Dedicated to the one I love.

STEVE PERRY

A singer's journey

by

Laura Monica Cucu

The unauthorized biography

Laura Monica Cucu contact info:
E-mail: spbook2006@yahoo.com

Original Steve Perry front cover photo by Mike Hausmann
Back cover photo by Vanessa Csucsi

This book is not approved or endorsed by Mr. Steve Perry, Journey, their management or label.

Thanks

I would like to thank my wonderful family for their immense love and support. I would have never made it without their help.

Vanessa and Paul, Laura and Didu - I love you.

Also, I would like to thank a few people who are very close to my heart:

To Marion Biering from Germany for being such a wonderful devoted friend.

To all my precious friends in the US: Mindy, Susan, Jodi, Kate, Noel, Mary, Jan, Kay, Sallee, Gayle, Gini and Caryn .

I am blessed to know you all.

To Mr. Mike Hausmann – thank you so much for being such a classy gentleman.

Many thanks to Lora Beard, Joe Benson, Mitch Lafon and Andrew McNeice.

To Mrs. Carol Felsenthal – thank you for all your priceless advices.

All my appreciation to Mr.George Frantu for his unreserved help and support.

Million thanks to Miki for the technical assistance.

My gratitude goes out to all the amazing people who helped me one way or the other throughout my work – I will always cherish your efforts and kindness.

Last but not least, I would like to thank the one and only Mr. Steve Perry for the music and the inspiration.

Introduction

Why a book about Steve Perry?

Why not? He is one of the greatest voices that music of all times ever had and for a long time he was the lead singer of one of the best American bands in rock music's history: Journey.

Steve Perry is a comprehensive artist and is considered a living legend - throughout three decades of constant changes in music, his name gained timeless power.

The first time I heard Steve Perry singing I immediately knew he was a different kind of an artist. The quality and uniqueness of his voice, the feelings and the sincerity conveyed in his performance, not to mention his first-class vocal style were absolutely fascinating. I was looking at a one-of-a-kind artist.

Because of my line of work I have listened to all kinds of music over the years and I've heard hundreds of singers of all genres. But soon, having the example of Steve Perry, I realized that the art of singing is something that only few musicians master.

This is a book about one of those very few. It is my tribute to an artist who inspired and swept away generations of people.

Steve Perry's career is also a testimony that dreams can come true if you really believe in what you are doing. It is a lesson of ambition, hard work, commitment, tenacity, passion, faith and love…Yes, it is all that and even more – it's about the bliss and the anguish of being wrapped up in fame, but in Steve Perry's case it's also a proof that only the strong ones pass the test of the double-edged sword called "stardom".

Artists are not the easiest people to decipher, but we must look at them with unadulterated eyes. There is no doubt that Steve Perry's artistic contribution to rock music is inestimable and his creativeness certainly stood the test of time; this singer wore his heart on his sleeve year after year in studios or on stage and this is how he made his way into the hearts of so many people around the world.

For anyone who wants to understand how could the gift of absolute talent be a blessing and a torture at the same time, for anyone who wants to comprehend that real success comes with sweat, blood and tears, this is a book that will reveal all that by going through the public life of one of the greatest lead singers of all times.

After you read it, take a moment and listen to Steve Perry singing. I am sure you will understand that real music comes straight from the heart.

Laura Monica Cucu

Contents

"Don't be afraid to run alone"

Steve Perry

"Cupid, draw back your bow

And let your arrow go

Straight to my lover's heart for me, for me..."

When the little boy heard that voice singing he almost stopped breathing.

He's been playing around with the car stereo's buttons listening to bits and pieces of so many songs, but now...this station was playing the most beautiful melody he'd ever heard ....And that voice, that soulful voice...was just magic.

He turned over to his mother who was driving and he asked:*" Who is that, Mom?"* She looked at her son with a sweet smile and she said:*"That's Sam Cooke."*

The little boy didn't say a word and continued listening to that voice in awe. His mother's Thunderbird was cruising down the street in Southern California's beautiful Pismo Beach, but he wasn't paying attention to anything around him...He was under the spell of the Music.

Something like a message coming from nowhere, made him close his eyes...*"That's what I want to do"*, he thought,*"I want to sing"*.

The year was 1961 and the boy's name was Steve Perry.

Searching For The Music

How could anyone fully understand something that only God knows how it's created? How could someone put into plain words the mystery of a talent that amazed generations of people all over the world?

Things like that are hard to describe and they sure can't be categorized because they have a class of their own. They say that miracles can only be witnessed.

When Steve Perry decided he wanted to sing, he had no idea what was planned for him. Now, after almost thirty years since he stepped on stage as a lead singer, we all know.

Music needed a Voice and that Voice graced the world with its beauty and warmed people's hearts with the sound of true music.

*

Let's travel back in time to California, somewhere in the San Joaquin Valley, in the small city of Lemoore where the young Steve Perry was enjoying his teenage years going to high school, hanging out with friends, listening to Sam Cooke or Marvin Gaye and trying to learn to play the drums. 1966 was the year when the band Cream made its debut with the album "Fresh Cream" – Steve Perry would confess later that he got hooked on Cream's music and he was listening to them all the time; then in 1967 Aretha Franklin's "Respect" was played on every FM station and the Beach Boys made everyone giddy with "Good Vibrations". But the one who rocked Steve Perry's world in a special way was Jimi Hendrix – the guitar genius made his wild psychedelic entrance in 1967 with his band, The Jimi Hendrix Experience, and with the "Are You Experienced?" album. From that point, the sound of music changed and Steve was witnessing everything. Three decades after that moment, he confessed that Jimi Hendrix's music will always have the power to take him back to that era, in a time filled with wonderful memories.

All through high school, Steve Perry was entirely captivated by music and that was pointed out in his looks as well: people were turning their heads when he passed by because of his shiny long dark hair which clearly revealed his love for rock`n`roll; although he was a shy guy, he had a passionate heart and his intense hazel-green eyes were sometimes speaking better than a thousand words. Steve was different from the other kids his age. Not only he had big dreams in which he believed, but he was pretty much aware that he possessed a special singing voice.

Being a teenager, he was mindful about his looks – he had a unique nose which brought him the nickname "Beaky Peartree" during high school years, as he amusingly confessed later. "Peartree" was the English word for "Pereira", his family's original name. Later, in one of his interviews, Steve said that his nose didn't bother him at all as he considered it his most interesting physical feature. Then he added: *"I believe God gave me this nose to sing"*.

Steve`s mother, Mary, was brought to America as a baby through Ellis Island by her parents Rose and Manuel Quaresma who moved to the United States from beautiful Pico Island, in the Azores Archipelago of Portugal. On the 22nd of January 1949, Mary's first and only child came into this world in the small town of Hanford, in central San Joaquin Valley, California. He was the first American born child in the Quaresma-Perrera family and at six months of age he was baptized Stephen Ray Perry at The Heart of Mary Church in Hanford.

Even though Steve was born and raised in the United States, his roots were strongly placed into Latinity both on the inside and outside; it was in his typical Portuguese looks as well as in his sensitive but yet naturally passionate nature. He grew up speaking both English and Portuguese and was influenced by these countries traditions in his everyday life. This double heritage made him express himself in a distinctive way and provided him the stamina to use the remarkable artistic nature he was born with.

One of Steve's childhood memories goes back to the time when he was only a five year old kid. It was Christmas time and the whole family was gathered at his grandmother's house. Steve thought about entertaining them the best way he could so he got this idea of putting together a little show. There was a big archway between the rooms and he came up putting some sheets over the archway to make it look like a stage curtain. Then he set up a record player and got out from behind the "curtain" lip-synching some songs in front of his very first audience. He remembers amused how his grandfather, who spoke broken English, was shouting:*" Louder! I can't hear ya!"* Then, after his performance, Steve would get a round of applause from all his relatives and that made him feel like he was a little star already! Also, his grandfather kept another memory from the days when Steve was just a little boy, as Steve himself remembers:*" My grandfather told me I was only three or four and I was singing with the radio, I was in his car and suddenly he hit the breaks because somebody jumped in front of the car and I flew forward and cut my head and the blood was dripping down my nose...but I kept singing!"*

Growing up in a family that was involved in show business, Steve discovered that music made him feel comfortable. He was always an enthusiastic radio listener and he would spend hours listening to all the artists of the era like Nat King Cole, Chuck Berry, The Platters, then Little Richard, Fats Domino and The Everly Brothers , just to mention a few. Who would've thought that one day Steve would go up on a stage and sing with The Everly Brothers themselves! But back then, in the 50s, Steve was only singing along with the radio. Fortunately, no one in his family was upset to hear him sing all the time and that was an inspirational thing for this young boy who wanted to find out what the meaning of music in his life was. He remembered later:*" I was obsessed with music when I was a kid. I came from a musical family -- my father was a big band singer and my mother was a dancer -- so my parents encouraged my interest in music. They bought me a drum kit, and they didn't yell at me when I'd sing in the shower."* Then he recalls another episode: *"When I was very young, the Dick Clark Caravan of Stars came to the San Joaquin Valley. It was James Brown, The Drifters, everybody. I was so little that my mother wouldn't let me go and she wouldn't take me."*

The only child of the Perry family was constantly preoccupied by music and he was very happy to have his own set of bongos – those were the first instruments that he ever played around the age of six; then his parents bought him a drum set when he was eight years old.*" I ended up having a drum set in my home in the San Joaquin Valley",* he recalled, *"and I ended up totally stuffing it with paper so I could play it. That killed some of it, but it didn't help the cymbals. I never thought to tape the cymbals but I didn't want to because then they wouldn't ring. That was my beginning on slamming and grooving."*

Another vivid childhood memory envisions his father, Raymond, singing on a theater stage - a moment that Steve will never forget; the sensation of "that's where I belong" was already there. He looks back at himself being just a tiny kid, wearing sandals, a sports coat and shorts, watching his father:*" I was three years old, and I was sitting in the front row of an auditorium in my hometown, and my grandmother was sitting with me and my mother was on stage because she was a dancer in this play. My dad was singing an Al Jolson kind of thing. I remember looking down at my little legs hanging, and looking up at him singing, and I knew that whatever I felt when he sang, inside of me I had that in there too. I knew I could do it. "*

Steve's father was his icon, the strong character that offered him protection. He never forgot all the nights when being just a little kid, his father used to sing him to sleep. Steve also remembers being afraid of wide roads and how his father would take his tiny hand and get him to the other side of the road in safety – that along with other moments remained etched in Steve`s memory , especially because his father left when he was seven years old. As he confessed later, that was one of the first major heartbreaking events in his life and to this day he believes that music eased the pain and helped him survive. Despite all the changes in his family life, Steve wasn't left alone in his artistic aspirations: his mother Mary was always there believing in him and his dreams. He remembers the way she would uphold him: *"She was always supportive from the very beginning when I was really young; I turned to her when I was very young and said 'Mommy I want to be a movie 'tar', and so she supported me through that cause. Her father, my grandpa, who was kind of the controlling force of the family said at first "What the hell you talkin' about?" He wanted me to be a farmer, but I just couldn't hang the idea of milking cows. "* Steve also remembers with amazing clarity a mysterious moment that was close to some kind of a prediction about what was going to happen in his life: *"Mom told me when I was 4 years old, to think of what it would feel like to live my dream. I saw cobalt colored lights mixed with red and a bright spotlight shining at me from across a large room. And then....There I was years later, really doing what I dreamed of doing. Total magic… it was total magic!!"*

It took twenty-five years until his childhood dream came through just as he imagined that day and his mother was going to be there to witness his triumph.

Steve`s early memories are still fresh: *"When I was seven years old my Mom put me in a Barber Shop Quartet. We would sing at all the local functions and later I was in different choirs. I then jumped quickly to being a drummer-lead singer in an R&B band. We'd play all the after game dances all around the Valley."* A few years later, Mary was the one that gave her twelve year old son the most precious gift, her way of saying how much faith she had in her son's talent: the gold Eight Note pendant and necklace. Steve kept it as a good-luck charm and wore it all the time when he was on stage; later in his career the Note became one of his so well known trademarks along with the tuxedo tails and the leopard printed shirts.

After his father left, Steve's grandfather, Manuel, became an important adviser in the following years, helping his young grandson in every way. When Steve was fourteen years old, his Mom remarried with Marv Rottman, who taught Steve many useful things and turned into a great companion:*" It was great having a new dad, but it was greater to have a new 'buddy' too!"* Steve was loved and he certainly had all the support he needed in his family.

As a kid, Steve was restless and he sure was the rebel kind – his mother confessed at the time that her son was *"born in a hurry"* and that was a good definition for the hyperactive kid that she couldn't turn her back on not for a moment! Mary was always ready to leap in because of her son's continuous itchy feet and Steve himself remembers a lot of close to tragedy situations when his mother literally had to save his life. At the age of seven when Steve and his mother were visiting the Azores Islands off the coast of Morocco, he recalls being on the edge of this huge volcano crater, when his exploring game almost made him fall inside! Mary rushed to save her boy just like she did that other time when Steve climbed a rock in the open Ocean and got on the verge of falling into the deep waters! After rescuing him, Mary said to her son:*" You took twenty years off my life!"* Steve admitted he was a very active kid:*" My mother said my legs and fingers were always going. I'm like that rabbit in 'Alice in Wonderland' who's always looking at his watch – I'm always looking and wondering what I'd have to do next."*

Many silly adventures peppered Steve's childhood and one of them turned into another story to remember. It happened in an abandoned house where Steve and three of his friends, Judy, Doug and Rose, were shooting at hubcaps with their B-B guns. While dangerously playing like that, they smashed the window of a passing car! The driver stopped in shock; Steve and his friends tried to run away but the man caught them and took them to their parents! In two shakes, all four of them were broke as they had to pay for the damage with their own money savings. Steve swore he will never do something like that again and he apologized to his angered mother.

As years went by, Mary was not only Steve's guardian angel but also the wind beneath his wings all that time when he tried to find the right track to lead him to his personal artistic fulfillment. She witnessed his efforts when he was playing the drums and singing in different high school bands and when Steve put together a group named "The Sullies" and actually recorded an album that was distributed locally, his mother went further and took the part of the manager for her son's band. Mary knew that Steve had an immense creative potential so she convinced him to participate with The Sullies to the "Battle of the Bands "in Calaveras County. "The Sullies" won the contest, fighting eighty other bands!

Twenty years later, while filming the Raised On Radio Documentary, Steve came back to the very same place where he and his mother shared their first victory together….And there were so many more to come that not even Steve would have dared to dream about when he graduated Lemoore High School in 1967.

---

*

The end of the 60s found Steve in Visalia, California, at the College of the Sequoias. The shy boy had turned into a young man who was now more daring in pursuing his dreams. Meanwhile, he stopped playing drums because he realized that his voice was getting much better than his drumming skills. His vocal awareness was due to the fact that he joined the College's Choir – he knew that was the right place to practice on his vocal abilities. Steve became first tenor in the Choir and he admits that doing scales and working on his voice on an every day basis helped him a lot in his later evolution as a singer.

Steve was so much in love with music that at one point in his teen life, he thought about working as a DJ in a radio station. He was not only excited by the thought of having a radio show, but was also thinking that maybe having a job in the media would make it easier to get in touch with the record business. He started practicing his DJ skills at home using a tape recorder and lowering his voice like radio announcers did. When he actually got a chance to be a real DJ he went for it. *" Back then you had to have a third class license to be a DJ, so I went to San Francisco to try to take my test with the F.C.C. At the time I was about as bright as a pink plastic soap dish on a slide rule so I flunk the test."*

However, Steve wasn't too disappointed and he moved on trying to find a way to become a career singer. He had no idea then that it wasn't really just a matter of time until he'd succeed but it was more about the hard work that followed in order to get up there where he belonged: among the greatest artists of all times!

Starting a profession as a singer wasn't an easy thing to do and nothing was going to happen overnight. Steve's first connection with a touring band came about in the beginning of the 70s .It was a Canadian group called Privilege and they hired Steve as one of the two vocalists. They even recorded together a song called "Don't It Feel Good" which was released as a single and right after that they went on a Canadian tour, traveling around in a big funky bus and playing in all the major cities like Quebec and Montréal. In fact, that was Steve's first road tour but unfortunately, being a singer, he couldn't stand the extreme weather conditions and had to quit: *" We traveled across Canada that summer and were doing quite well, but when October rolled around we were someplace in northern Alberta and I left to come back to California. Man, it was just too cold for me up there!"*

Slowly but surely, Steve became conscious that the only way he could get closer to the point he wanted to reach was to move to Los Angeles, the restless City of the Angels that was a tempting place not only for movie makers and actors but for musicians as well. Recording studios, clubs, managers, producers, everybody and everything was there. Steve decided to give up the Visalia College and become an L.A. resident. First thing he did was to find work, so occasionally he was lending his vocals to radio and TV commercials. This was a way of making a living, but meanwhile he was trying to get closer to the people in the music industry. In just a few months after he moved to Los Angeles he had already met and worked with a bunch of musicians but quickly got disappointed by the lack of motivation that some of these people had:*" Their minds were not career-oriented"*, he said, *"They were partying musicians and not thinking further than that. Everytime I turned around they would be late, not show up for rehearsals…that kind of thing"*. Steve had a clear vision of what he wanted: a musical statement, to the state-of-the-art of a musician. He admitted later:*" I was looking for the perfect rock and roll band - a band that never existed and probably never will."* All these goals were hard to reach and meanwhile Steve had to pay his bills. He had no problem confessing later that he was starving in Los Angeles and he didn't quite have money for anything else but food.

While worrying with everyday life, Steve decided that the next best place for him would be a studio, especially because he was fascinated by the technical part of the recording process. That's how he ended up working for two years as a second engineer and tape operator at Crystal Studios in L.A., a job that took him even closer to the musical acts of the era. The producer working there was also a sound engineer so after hours Steve would work with him and do vocals to try getting a demo. That was a great way for Steve to learn about a lot of studio procedures which helped him later to have a clear idea on the way his songs should sound. This job at Crystal Studios was also a good way for him to notice that the people who were coming to record were already together as bands. Then Steve realized that standing behind the glass kept him away from his dream. He remembers those times: *"Working at Crystal Records kept me alive for a while but found out it was taking time away from what I was doing musically. I got a lot of exposure as to what was going on and I thought that was better than nothing. But I felt like I was sort of spinning my wheels… so I got out."*

By the end of the 70s, Steve met drummer Craig Krampf and in 1977 along with musicians Lee Stephens, Steve Delacy and Richard Michaels they put together a rock band named Alien Project. They started writing and recording songs and soon enough a great demo was put together. No one could've imagined that one of those songs, called "If You Need Me, Call Me" was destined to make all the difference in Steve's life! But at that point, Alien Project seemed to be the band which would give Steve the chance to express himself the way he wanted to and lead him towards the career he was trying to build. He was feeling very comfortable with them and there was an obvious musical drive that kept them going in the right direction." *They were a pure rock and roll band"*, Steve said, *"yet they had a style that allowed me to stretch out as a singer."* Things began to move faster and soon the band had a great perspective as Craig Krampf said*:" When the four of us played it was magic! We were like six hours old when Chrysalis and Columbia wanted to sign us!"*

Then came the 4th of July, 1977.America was celebrating Independence Day. Steve and his band mates were happy and excited that Alien Project was going to sign a record deal in the days to come. Unfortunately, everything changed that very day. Richard Michaels, the band's bass player was killed in a terrible car crash. Steve got a message that day about Richard's death and he was completely shocked not only because one of his best friends was gone but also because he realized that their dreams were shattered. Richard's death affected him so deeply that he felt like he couldn't keep on doing music with Alien Project because without his friend things would have not been the same. He was depressed and very confused: *"I didn't know what to do after that happened. Here I was - a singer without a band. Every musician's dream, a recording contract with a major label, gone as quickly as it was there... Where do you do from there?"*

They all decided to give up Alien Project.

Devastated and hopeless, Steve left Los Angeles and went back home to the San Joaquin Valley to get some comfort and strength in the arms of his family. He felt his dreams and hopes were out of his reach again and he was thinking that maybe he wasn't supposed to have what he was longing for.*" I threw my hands up to the sky and asked 'Why?'... I got the impression that somebody up there didn't want me to make it."*

Shortly after returning home, Steve was forced to reorganize his lifestyle and find a regular job in order to make a living. The best job he was offered was at the turkey ranch which his step-father Marv owned but it wasn't something he enjoyed doing.*" I hated it"*, he said,*" I was building sheds and doing other odd jobs, but I confess that I learned a lot about working with my hands and about how important it is to take pride in your work."* After many years, in an interview, Steve confessed with humor that he will never forget the frustrating times he went through while he worked at the ranch being surrounded by hundreds of gobbling turkeys – the sounds was annoying him to the point where he swore he will never have a turkey dinner in his life again!

Caught up in that new living situation, it looked like Steve was giving up on music. But somewhere inside his heart he was hoping that maybe one day he will find the zeal to start all over again.

Meanwhile, in one of the Columbia Records offices, a manager by the name of Herbie Herbert was listening to a demo tape which he got from a friend of his who was working at CBS.It was a recording made by a band called Alien Project and the song he was listening to was "If You Need Me, Call Me" .It was one of the many tapes he received after spreading the word that he was looking for a good lead singer to front a rock band called Journey which he was managing. The members of the band were Gregg Rolie, Neal Schon, Ross Valory and Ainsley Dunbar. Journey was around since 1973 and they were touring most of the time back and forth across the country, playing as an opening act for everyone from Aerosmith to Kiss, or performing as special guests for Electric Light Orchestra.

Journey had already done a few albums but they weren't getting enough attention. The fusion prog-rock they were playing wasn't getting them on the radio either. In those times if a band wasn't heard on the FM stations, the chances of becoming successful were close to zero. At on point, Journey got a harsh ultimatum from their record company: if they won't change things in their music they will be fired. It was then when Herbie Herbert decided that his band needed to take a different direction, a vocally hit-oriented style that would get them radio airplay and record buyers. So he began searching for that special singer that could go well with Journey. And there he was! This singer he was listening to was incredibly gifted - he had an amazing voice range and a distinctive singing manner that impressed him. Interesting enough, Herbert was familiar with the name of Steve Perry, although he never heard him sing before; Herbert remembered meeting him a few times but back then he wasn't looking for a vocalist. Now it was different. Steve Perry was so good he couldn't believe his luck! After sixty seconds, he stopped the tape and made his decision.

Finally, Journey was going to have a Voice.

The Pearl In The Shell

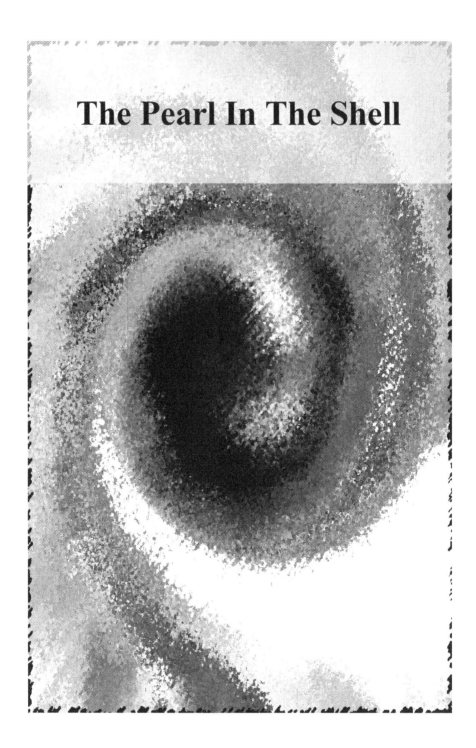

Sometimes life moves in mysterious ways. The strange part in how the greatest AOR band was put together was the fact that Steve knew about Journey since that night when he saw Neal Schon playing guitar in a club. He loved the sound of his guitar and his great skills and he even got to meet the entire band backstage. More, after the concert Steve and Neal had a long talk about music and Neal even gave Steve a ride home. Starting that night at the club, Steve knew he wanted to sing with Journey. But, as he confessed later, he thought: *" How do you walk up to someone and say 'Hey, I wanna sing in your band' when they're already happy with their singer?"* Just then, Journey was trying to get used to the idea of having a lead singer. His name was Robert Fleischman and he would occasionally add his vocals to some of the band's songs. Although it seemed that the lead singer's spot in the band was already taken, Herbie Herbert wanted something different.

When Herbert listened to Steve Perry's demo tape and called him that day, history began writing itself. In one of his later interviews, Steve mentioned that phone call as being one of the most precious memories of his career. Herbert told him about the demo song he just heard and that he was looking for a lead singer to front Journey. Steve remembers: *" He asked me to fly out to Denver, Colorado, to meet and hang with the band."* However, before leaving to meet Journey, Steve was still having doubts, so he turned to his grandfather Manuel for advice. He recalls the conversation with him:*" I said 'You know Grandpa, I don't know if I'm supposed to be in this business 'cause every time I get this much closer something equally as big comes and knocks it down"*. Mr. Quaresma's answer went straight to the point:*" I don't know much about this music business you're in, but these Journey guys, I think they have jobs, and you need a job"*. Lastly, Steve was set in motion by his mother. When he told her that maybe he should be better off without music she didn't agree.*" She was amazing"*, remembers Steve,*" she said 'No, don't give up yet, something will happen out of this, you don't know yet."*

That's how Steve finally flew out to Denver and spent some time on the road with Journey watching everything from the wings. Herbie Herbert introduced Steve to everyone as being the Portuguese cousin of John Villanueva, one of Journey's road crew members. The band was still touring with singer Robert Fleischman but Herbert had already plans to replace him.

The manager knew that it was going to be hard to change things and that the band members were going to have a tough time adjusting to the new situation. But he had a good instinct and he was convinced that Steve Perry will lead the band into the right direction. It was only a matter of time until Steve and the rest of the band would blend together and get things rolling. Yet, Neal Schon, the guitarist, was the stubborn one. When Herbie told him that Steve Perry had a good chance of becoming the new singer of Journey, Neal wasn't too happy. He still wasn't convinced that Journey needed a lead singer; he wanted to jam and have his own way of expressing himself. But Herbie Herbert wouldn't negotiate with any of them as he was more than determined to change the band's musical approach and bring in Steve Perry as the lead singer.

One day, during a sound check in Long Beach, Herbert made sure Fleischman was going to be busy that afternoon, then he brought in Steve and put together a rehearsal session with the rest of the band. When Steve took the microphone in his hand he had the feeling that those guys were not too content to have him there and that they were expecting him to fail this test. Sure, they've heard his demo tape, but somehow they didn't really believe that he could sing like that in a live situation. The pressure was so high Steve had to close his eyes. The only way he could make it was to let his deep musical emotion take over. He knew the lyrics of the song they were supposed to play together, so he started singing "For You", an unreleased Journey song. Steve`s crystal clear voice filled the place with so much intensity it was breathtaking. The notes were flowing effortlessly, pouring purity into everyone's ears. The personnel of the arena, the ushers and the stage workers came from all over the place just to listen to this man singing. They were all so impressed with his performance that when Steve finished the song they gave him a standing ovation! The band members looked at each other in surprise - they'd never heard anyone singing like that before on a stage. This man holding the microphone was out of this world! For a long time no one said anything but then the guys wanted to try another song and then another…They were already sensing a connection between them which was impossible to ignore. On that day it was decided that Steve would join the band. Robert Fleischman was out of the group very soon after that.

Steve recalls very clearly the exact situation when he and Neal wrote their first song together. After Steve arrived in Denver, they were staying in a hotel room and Neal was playing the acoustic guitar for fun when he came up with this beautiful melody – it was an opening line for what later turned into one of the most beloved songs in Journey's career. Steve got inspired by the soulful sound of Neal's guitar and he wrote down some words. Then one thing led to another and in less than an hour the song was done. It was called "Patiently".

From that moment on, for many years to come, Steve would get inspired by Neal's special way of playing and all the way through Journey's history Steve's voice and Neal's guitar became inseparable and complementary just like *"salt and pepper"*. Steve confessed later:*" The way he played guitar, the sound and the heart behind his guitar…I just had a kinship with it that was deeper than I could explain."* The instant musical chemistry between Steve and Neal was unbelievable. They would write songs all the time whenever they felt like it: on the road, in hotels, during rehearsals or backstage before concerts. Steve was also a good bass player and he started writing songs and bringing them to the band. That's how one night, backstage at the Swing Auditorium in San Bernardino, Steve played this unfinished song he had been working on. It was called "Lights" and the next minute the whole band was harmonizing along with him. It didn't take too much for the song to be completed and soon after that "Lights" became not only one of the most popular songs in the world but it turned into one of San Francisco's greatest anthem-like tunes. Funny enough, this song wasn't supposed to be about San Francisco in the beginning. Steve had another city in mind. It was Los Angeles and the original words were *"when the lights go down in the city and the sun shines on LA"*, but Steve wasn't happy with that outcome*: "I didn't like the way it sounded at the time and I just had it sitting back in the corner. Then when I got in Journey and spent a lot of time in San Francisco, I changed it."* He also remembers perfectly the inspirational image behind the song: *"We were coming up from the L.A. area to San Francisco. This friend and I got this big truck and loaded up my apartment. We were going across the Golden Gate Bridge and it was one of those early mornings going across the bridge things when the sun was coming up and the lights were going down. It was perfect."*

Steve's heart belonged now to the City by the Bay and "Lights" was his proof of love for the place he was already calling home. But by the end of August 1977 Steve had one more place to call home: Journey.

*

If there is a significant moment which Steve will always remember that would be the night of October 28th, 1977 when he stepped on stage with Journey for the first time as the new lead singer of the band. It happened at the Old Waldorf in San Francisco in front of something like six thousand people. But those people were there to hear the progressive instrumental music that Journey played at the time and they didn't understand what was that new feathered-hair guy doing on stage singing about some city lights and why did Journey changed their sound so dramatically! At first, the audience hated Steve. He confessed that he felt people's negative response immediately so he didn't move too much because of all that nervous tension he was experiencing. *"That was a frightening show because I was thrown out in front of the die-hard fans that didn't want to see nobody out there, you know..."* Then he recalls amused: *"I saw a lot of middle fingers back then. I'm glad I was fit enough to dodge the beer bottles thrown at me onstage."* He wasn't quite the entertainer that night but something else was there, making people calm down and listen: his voice. All dressed up in white, gracefully holding the microphone, Steve sang with his pure high-pitched voice and did what felt it was best: he allowed music to take over, opened his heart to the ones listening to him and delivered all the soulfulness of his voice into his performance. It wasn't too long before everyone was charmed. After the show was over, some of the people in the audience said that they believed they've heard an angel singing.

When Steve Perry and the band got off stage it was all clear: this was the new Journey.

The pearl had found its shell.

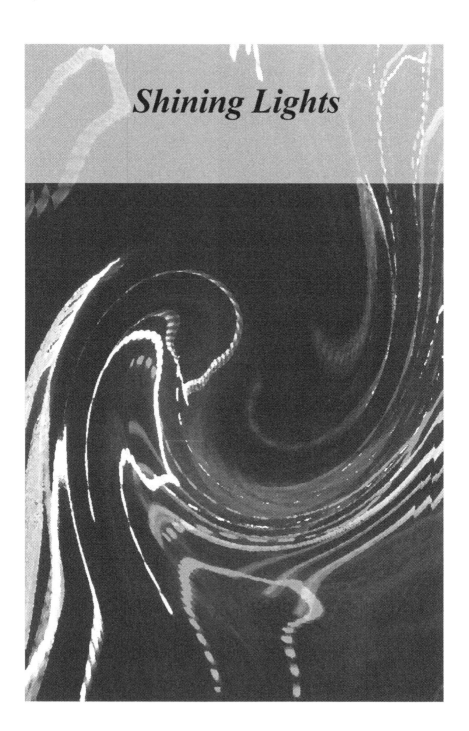

Shining Lights

It was like Steve and his new partners have discovered together the very source of genuine music. Whenever they'd start writing songs, there was a magical creative energy between them that would bring out some incredible ideas. It was a new fresh sound, a distinctive combination of sweet harmonies and hard rocking riffs that turned out to be a true musical revolution of the times. That first short tour they did together confirmed the fact that they really had a strong musical confluence going on, both on and off stage, and more, intuition told them that they were set to do great things together. When asked about his very first tour with Journey, Steve recalled how some of the people in the audience only wanted to listen to the songs from the first three Journey albums. However, it wasn't that hard to win them over as Steve said:*" It was really wild, but before the night was over everybody came to appreciate the new stuff"*.

When that tour ended, Journey already had enough material for an album so they hook up with a renowned producer who was working with the British superstars of Queen: Thomas Roy Baker. Steve was looking forward to work with Baker, especially because he was impressed with Queen's stellar evolution. As a matter of fact, Steve had a vivid memory about the first Queen concert he saw before becoming Journey's singer. In a recent interview, he recaptured the feelings he experienced then: *"I had never seen such a performance before. It was truly a larger-than-life moment to see Freddie Mercury with his powerful operatic vocals, and the band, and Brian May's guitar. The whole thing was just massive for me. I think that was a moment when I felt in my heart that I can do this."*

Back in 1977 it was Steve's turn to live his dream - by the end of that year he entered His Masters Wheels Studio in San Francisco and started working with Journey on their first album together. The studio wasn't one of the best the band could've asked for; it was a moderately equipped basement, but it was working fine for them. That until the day when they all decided to celebrate a perfect guitar solo and the whole thing degenerated into a foam bath as Baker played around with the studio's fire extinguishers! What started off as an innocent party ended up being a technical tragedy: the studio equipment was covered with a corrosive layer of foam and although Baker did a fine job cleaning up the mess, the place had to be abandoned for good. Journey relocated at Cherokee Studios, in Southern California's Beverly

Hills, to be able to finish off the recordings for the new album. Roy Thomas Baker certainly knew how to have some wild fun when he felt like it, however, he knew how to keep focused on the production and the sound of the album. One of the interesting parts was that in the mixing process Baker decided to "play" with the left and right channels, then highlighted some of the sounds, separated others and made songs like "Feeling That Way/Anytime" to gain a special resonance; all in all the "Infinity" album is considered to this day a ground-breaking record and, for the ones who like to savor the sounds, a must listen on headphones.

"Infinity" was Steve's moment - his very first meaningful musical statement that would give him the chance to share his astounding talent and musical vision with the world. He wanted to be able to record the songs at his best – indeed, time would prove that those ten songs were made to become masterpieces that would add a new chapter in rock music's records. With Steve's exceptional touch, Journey was rocking in a way that made people get hooked forever. Nevertheless, not only the listeners were astounded by Journey's new singer but musicians as well. Over the years, Steve turned out to be the voice that influenced many vocalists from Jimi Jamieson of Survivor to James LaBrie of Dream Theater and even modern Latino singers like Ricky Martin. Steve's breathtaking rendition on "Something to Hide", one of his all time favorite songs, wasn't only a soul stirring performance but it also set a new vocal standard among rock singers to this very day. Time would confirm that Steve Perry was in a league of its own and his vocal capabilities were set to remain unmatched.

On the 8th of January 1978, the" Infinity" album was released in a world that was craving for musical changes. Journey was already there delivering to the listeners something different and the key of their new sound was Steve's dazzling vocals doubled by Neal Schon's remarkable guitar creativity. People were fascinated with Steve's unusual voice - he simply melted hearts because of the way he was delivering the songs; all in all, "Infinity" brought clusters of new fans into the Journey camp and many of them admitted that once they've heard Steve Perry sing they were irremediably captivated. The impact of the album was tremendous and the main question on everyone's lips was: "Who is this man singing like that? Who is Steve Perry?" Not only were the fans thrilled, but Steve's family as well. After many years, in one of his interviews, he recalled what was one of the most touching moments in his career, an emotional story about his relative's reaction to Infinity's success:*" A cousin of mine called me on the phone and said:' I saw your mom the other day, your first album," Infinity", came out and she had it on an 8 track and she put it in the car and said to me 'Listen to this!' And my mom pulled my cousin in the car and turned it up!".* Steve humorously added: *"So my mom was pulling relatives off the street saying 'Get in the car, listen to this, this is my son!'"*

Step by step, Steve began to reveal his artistic persona and skills by performing every night in front of huge audiences. His stellar voice filled the stadiums and made people feel and understand that they were witnessing a phenomenon. His unique vocal style was immediately noticed in the rock industry and he began being nominated for the most significant awards. He was truly touched by very emotional episode back in the days, at one of the Bammy Awards ceremony he attended in San Francisco at the end of the 70s, when he was up for the "Vocalist Of The Year" award. It happened right before the show started and an orchestra played an overture of all the songs of that year. Steve remembers: *"As I was coming up the hallway to get back to my seat, they got to the part where they were playing "Lights" and I never heard my melody on an orchestra before! It choked me to where I could barely breathe, and I was emotionally on the border of losing it. I didn't win that year, but I won five years in a row the next year."*

The first headline concert of the Infinity Tour was held in Chicago with an 1800-seat sold out show at the Riviera Theater. A few months later, Journey got back to Chicago and played in front of four thousand people at Aragon Hall. In the following nine moths of touring, Journey returned to perform in Chicago eleven times. They definitely were the city's heroes! Chicago was also the place where Journey got to be on the same stage with The Rolling Stones for the first time. Mick Jagger's band was a huge name in the industry and Journey accepted to sing as an opening act. But things turned out a little bit different than The Rolling Stones might've expected. Steve recalled in a later interview a somewhat amusing situation on that hot day of July 8, 1978 at the Soldiers Field arena: *"I'll never forget we've opened the show for the Rolling Stones...and they were big. But they didn't know that Journey had been in Chicago many times and Chicago was the place that Journey was already selling big arenas, bigger than anywhere else in America. We did really well that night....Eighty thousand people liked it, we did two encores and the Rolling Stones waited a long time before they could come on stage... They really waited a long time."*

All the way through the United States, millions of men and women would line up for days to catch the best tickets for the Journey concerts. They wanted to hear the new music. They wanted to hear that Voice. Every single time Steve walked on the stage he had the tenacity to be the best he could be: *"(...) The goal was to reach large stadiums and to play such venues and have all those people know for once and for all that maybe you're pretty good at what you do."* He was aware of his gift and fortunately, his voice was keeping up with his extreme demands: *"You know, I was really asking a lot of it and it was going along with the ride."*

Many of those who sat in the audience in those times remember the incredible feelings they'd get when Steve was singing. His live vocal rendition was beyond belief; the energy, the driving force of the entire band and the way Steve would interact with the audience were making people get a "high" feeling that, as many stated, *"...would last for days after the concert"*. No one could explain exactly how Steve was capable of touching them so deeply, but it was clear that his vibrant emotional voice was causing serious addiction. His charisma was also something unforgettable. Later, when asked about the way people responded to his stage presence, he said: *"I guess I look vulnerable, that's why people react to me."*

Steve was getting more and more confident on stage; his relationship with the audience grew stronger with every concert – it looked like he was a natural born entertainer and now he had the right place and the right music to inspire him to be the best.

The tour turned out to be a huge success and made Journey a top name in the music industry. By October 10, 1978, the "Infinity" album went Platinum. It was Journey's first triumph but there wasn't too much time to savor it as the band was on the road month after month and they were all working very hard. However, touring was something that Steve did with passion because he just couldn't live without this anymore. He admitted that sometimes he felt more comfortable on the road than at home and there were times when he even forgot where home was. He recalls the grueling parts of his job: *"The Infinity tour went on for one hundred and eighty-five shows back-to-back. We were the hardest touring band. We would stay out there. I was coming back to my Mom's house because I didn't even have an apartment yet. I remember the phone rang one Christmas and I leaped out the bed and I ran down the hall thinking I was late for the bus. I mean I would reach for the phone and dial 9 for a line out. I knew that I had been on the road too long."*

At one point Steve's complete abandon and commitment to the tour schedule brought up some health problems that he had no idea they were developing. He bears in mind a time when he had to go see a doctor mid-tour because he noticed his voice was getting somewhat powerless. He found out he had walking pneumonia and, if not for the fact he was young and in good health, chances were that he just might have not woken up one morning! The gravity of the situation shocked him: *"I said 'wha-aaa-at?!' I couldn't believe it. I started thinking about what that meant, and that if I was going to die it would have been in St. Louis where I was at my sickest and the tour was at its heaviest. Luckily I found out in time and got better."* But despite his critical condition, Steve went up on stage at the Checker Dome and performed like he always did: flawless.

During the Infinity Tour Steve had to go through a weird situation that occurred because their tour sound engineer wanted to become a recording engineer and he suddenly decided to leave Journey and the tour. It was a tricky situation, as they didn't have anyone to fill in and do the job. But Steve had a good experience from his time as a studio engineer at "Crystal Studios" so it wasn't hard for him to take over the chores to some extent. But how could he be at the mixing board and then sing on stage the same night? In a recent interview, Steve explained amused how they worked things out:"*We would set everything up during sound check, so when the show started all I had to do was to walk out there with my Levi's on and my t-shirt and my long hair and unmute my mike. Then Gregg Rolie would be starting 'Opened my eyes to a new kind of way' and I would stand in the wings and I would grab my mike and walk on stage!*"

*

Shortly after the Infinity Tour started, Journey already had national acknowledgment, a growing fan base and a road paved with platinum records. It was more than this band could've dreamed of. But the fame and the fortune weren't their major interests - they were so focused on their music that they'd write songs all the time. Most of them were written collectively on the road, while traveling from town to town; some of the best songs came out from Steve's personal experiences - he would come up with a melody and finish the song with Neal in perfect harmony. Before they knew it they had material for a new album so they didn't waste any time. Thomas Roy Baker was put in command again for the production part of the "Evolution" album – eleven songs were recorded in 1979 at the same studio in Beverly Hills where "Infinity" was cut. But at one point, during the recording sessions for "Evolution", Steve got the impression that Baker wasn't working the way he was supposed to and that, as a producer in charge, he did nothing really special except for multi-track. Steve noticed that Baker wouldn't hang out too much with the band; he was just coming and going in the studio and wouldn't be concerned too much with the meticulous production process. By comparison, Steve was aware that Baker had been more involved in the "Infinity" album and when it came to "Evolution" he wasn't providing that positive feedback that the band needed from a producer. But all in all Steve was happy with the way "Evolution" came out because he and the band got completely involved in all the stages of the recording. He admitted: *" We pulled it through. We did it ourselves ".*

Along with the "Evolution" project, Journey's line-up changed with drummer Ainsley Dunbar's departure. His feeling was that the new Journey music was too simple for him and his musical background demanded him to play in a more majestic progressive way. His skills were excellent but his style was too complicated for Journey's new musical approach; Dunbar felt it would be better for everyone to let his position available for a more appropriate drummer. After Dunbar left, in came Steve Smith – a very gifted drummer who immediately complemented Journey's sound. All five of them were perfectly harmonized with each other and that's why throughout the years the fans and the critique would name this formula Journey's *"golden line-up"*. Smith admitted back in the days: *"It really was a decision that came knowing these guys as people and friends. I love the way that Steve sings and I love the way Neal plays guitar. I felt like I really wasn't satisfied of doing the things I've done before joining Journey. I wanted to learn new things."* Right from the beginning, Steve had a close musical relationship with the new drummer and felt that he could easily pull out the songs with Smith's special drumming abilities: *"Steve Smith was playing in a manner that was absolutely hard to describe, with a true fervor and vengeance to his playing and I can see that that kind of drive that he had made it possible for me as the singer to sit in the back seat of him driving in the front, and just soar"*. When asked about how he felt working in the studio with Steve Perry, Smith evoked the recording sessions for "Evolution", especially the moment when Steve taped the vocals for "Sweet and Simple". He remembers watching Steve through the glass of the recording booth and having the feeling that he was witnessing perfection. Steve's voice moved him deeply and he confessed that he'd never heard anyone before singing like Steve did. By watching him working on the vocal part of "Sweet and Simple", Smith realized that Steve Perry was a true perfectionist: if he felt he didn't pull out a certain note like he wanted to, he'd stop and do it all over again until he'd reach the perfect sound. "Sweet and Simple" was one of those songs that Steve wanted to be impeccable, so he kept stopping, going back and re-recording parts of it several times. Smith was impressed: *"I was looking at him, listening to that stunning voice and thinking 'This man is out of this world'. All the others left; it was just Steve and me in the studio. I couldn't go away, I couldn't move."*

"Sweet and Simple" was a song that Steve had written five years before joining Journey and the music just came into his mind while contemplating the beauty of Lake Tahoe. It was a beautiful, tender love song with a stupendous vocal line that became not only a timeless classic rock ballad but furthermore a voice class for lots of singers. After many years, Steve was asked about the recording process and about the way he perceived the songs he was recording in the studio back then: *"There was always something in me that told me 'that's the one, that's the song'. I've always listened to that. Whatever that is in me that resonates and says 'that take is ready' or 'that take is not quite there' "*

The entire "Evolution" album was a triumph. "Lovin`, Touchin`, Squeezin`" - a song that Steve wrote all by himself, would become the first Billboard Top 20 single in Journey's history. This song was a true story that Steve had gone through at one point when he saw his girlfriend at the time getting out of this fancy Corvette and giving the driver a long kiss. He was looking at the whole scene through the window of his house and he never forgot that experience. Later he wrote "Lovin`, Touchin`, Squezin' and named it *"a love justice song"*. This tune became one of the most recognizable Journey musical marks to this day and fans got to even count the "nah, nah, nah"- s that Steve sings towards the end of the song: 154 times!

On the 18th of February 1979, Journey recorded the video for "Lovin`, Touchin`, Squeezin`"" in front of a very cheerful audience and that one special video became a classic along with Steve`s famous red silk shirt and black spandex pants – the outfit of a genuine 70s rock star! Many years after, in a radio interview, Steve humorously confessed that he had a name for that red shirt: the *"diaphanous"* one.

By the time the video for "Lovin`, Touchin`, Squeezin` " was going into the production phase, the management was gearing up for the Evolution Tour that was planned to begin with a series of concerts in Europe starting April of 1979. But the band wasn't taking any time off. The guys were open minded and willing to play everything they wanted   – they would experiment new musical challenges as often as they could. That`s why when CBS Studios proposed Journey to do a King Biscuit Flower Hour radio broadcast, they accepted. The King Biscuit Flower Hour was presenting standard live sets of different famous bands of the time, but Journey wanted to do something different: they thought of an extravagant live project which included the Tower of Power horn section and background vocalists Annie Sampson and Jo Baker of Stoneground as well as guests like Tom Johnston of the Doobie Brothers. Steve was more than thrilled to be able to use his rhythm and blues roots and get a mixture of his vocal skills. For the first time since Steve was in Journey he tried out soul songs like Sam Cooke's "Good Times" or Sam and Dave's "Hold On, I'm Coming", as well as blues songs like Albert King's "Born Under A Bad Sign" and Robert Johnston's "Crossroads". The show was absolutely flamboyant and Journey revealed a new side which they wouldn't put on show too often in the years to come. Sadly enough, the recording of this unique concert was never released.

*

Steve knew exactly what he and Journey wanted to do at that time: *"We wanted to make a statement"*, he said, *"and it was a point to play everywhere, to let people know we had made a change, that they wouldn't be able to ignore us anymore. And they're not ignoring us!"* But some critics were not so pleased with Journey's success and kept calling them "commercial" or "corporate band". Those people were over analyzing and misjudging a natural writing skill that the band members had and were unable to see the beauty of the music that was touching millions of people. Steve was answering them with facts:" *Journey has a very broad-based appeal because our personalities and music cover a wide range. What have made me laugh all this time is when people have called us a "faceless band" yet there are twenty thousand fans at every show screaming our names!"*

Even so, Steve wasn't concerned about the disparagement the band had to face. When he was asked about the commercial sound of Journey's music, he stated: *"Commercial is a misused word. If you've got to tie it in a monetary value, I'd say 'successful' would be the word to use. And what's wrong with being successful?"* Then he added:" *Criticism doesn't make me feel bad, because I think that the people know; they like what we're doing."*

With "Evolution" completed and set to be released in July of 1979, the Journeymen embarked on a huge World Tour that would take them on the road for almost one year. But before that, the band was invited to perform and record a special show in Chicago. It was a very popular TV show called "Soundstage" which was featuring all the big artists of the era. The PBS series hosted remarkable names like Bob Dylan, Aretha Franklin, The Doobie Brothers, The Temptations, Bonnie Raitt and many others. All the concerts were filmed before small audiences and that gave the viewers at home the feeling of going through the show firsthand. Journey's performance from that summer of `79 was stellar and it added to their already massive popularity.

However, the band was looking forward to get on the road. The Evolution Tour was promising and Steve was going to experience something he wanted to do for a long time: singing on huge arenas! He confessed that he was completely overwhelmed when he sang on a stadium for the first time. Seeing something like 70.000 fans in front of him, hearing their response to the music and receiving their energy, all that just rocked his world! It was totally magic for him and it was for the first time when he truly understood that one of his childhood biggest dreams had come true!

This time, because of the way the Evolution Tour was planned, not only the American fans were getting to see Journey on stage. The band crossed the Atlantic and started their European tour in Manchester, England, where on the 21st of March they rocked the Apollo Theater; the band traveled from Germany to Scandinavia then to Japan and back – it was a power tour that allowed millions of people to understand that the world was blessed with the brilliance of a unique group of musicians. After getting back from Japan, the "Evolution" album had already reached Gold and Journey started their non-stop touring through the major US cities; the first concert was set for the 2nd of May 1979 in Medford, Oregon at the Jackson County Expo Center. Then there were all the big venues in Illinois, Ohio, Colorado, Texas, Arizona, California – every single corner of America was reached. Steve was experiencing the wonderful feeling of singing in front of massive audiences like in those amazing "Day on the Green" shows at the Oakland Coliseum Stadium or at the Cominskey Park in Chicago. During the "Evolution" Tour, Journey set a new attendance record in Detroit where forty-eight thousand fans came each night to see the band in four sold out shows over one weekend at Cobo Hall. Steve was bringing his magnificent voice out in the open and his range and strength kept growing with every concert. People started being curious about the ways he was getting in vocal shape for the concerts– it was obvious that such a striking vocal capacity needed a special regime. Steve was very honest about his hard work: *"I do at least a half-hour warm up every night before the show",* he confessed at the time. *"On the road it gets into achieving consistency. So if that means not speaking for a day, because I felt the night before I was getting a little ragged, or if we have worked six or seven nights in a row, then I do have to make up for it by not speaking and drinking more water."* Fortunately, Steve was conscious that he is the owner of a wonderful natural instrument that needed his full attention and care. *" I am not going to do anything that is going to make me unable to sing. I am not going to do anything to hurt my voice."* He began leading a self-disciplined lifestyle, but it was a very cruel professional timetable: rehearsals, voice warm-ups, working out, going to bed early, and then getting a certain vocal care that would allow him to perform at his best every night. He knew that a singer was in a more delicate situation than any other musician, because he had to deal with a biological instrument that couldn't be replaced like other instruments could. *" Your voice is all you are going to get",* he said, *"You are better off keeping what you have and make sure you have it for a while. That takes discipline and it's frustrating.* Steve acknowledged in one of his interviews back then: *" I try to do everything I do with the least amount of effort. For example on the song 'Wheel In The Sky' when the solo is going on, I am up there doing these angelic things. I use the least amount of effort to pull out these ideas. If they don't come out, they I don't go for them. But nine times out of ten, they come."*

Although Steve was quite the workaholic kind and being on the road was his best way to get inspired and keep in shape, at times he would start missing the peacefulness of his home. *"When you go on the road you have a limo driver, picks you up, drives you to the airport, then someone's flying you once you get to the airport, so you never get to drive anywhere…So when I get home sometimes I think I don't know how to drive (…) There's just a feeling of being home that you just can't explain…It's something you miss. You are in a hotel every night, a different hotel, different beds, different pillows, everything."*

Despite the fatigue, the guys knew how to have some fun for a change! Steve remembers a lot of crazy situations when they would get nervous or scared but have some good laughs as well! Like the limo incident in Detroit! The whole band was traveling in two fancy limousines and the traffic was very heavy. At one point, the driver of Steve's limo slammed into the car in front of them and because of the sudden stop, the other Journey limo behind them hit Steve's limo pretty hard! After the shock, they all got out of the two bashed-up luxury cars and started kicking them and jumping around! People from the other cars in the traffic were watching this unexpected show: five guys acting zany near two smashed limousines. Steve stated later:"*Oh, yeah, you get pretty crazy when you're out on the road awhile!*"

There were scary things happening not only in the limos but in planes as well! Steve had been always afraid of flying, but when touring all over across America he had no choice but endure the flights between the venues. He recalls spine-chilling episodes like this: "*We were on a DC-9 in Florida and we were about to take off - we were going very fast when the right engine blew, we veered to the side and came to a screeching halt! We got off and left an hour later with a different plane, but we were all still shaken!*" But the series of frightening flying situations didn't end there: "*Once we were on the runway and I noticed the bay door of the plane was open as we were about to take off! I hollered to the flight attendant and I figured she was going to think:' Why is this long-haired rock singer screaming?', but she quickly radioed the pilot, and he stopped the plane so the ground crew would close the door!*" Fortunately, the band got to the venues safe and sound everytime.

The fans were having a certain image about the members of Journey – they were considered huge rock stars and Steve was experiencing the fame and recognition coming along with that ticket. However, he wasn't acting like a big-time celebrity because focusing on his best performance was the most important thing. "*There's no way any of us can get big-headed.*", he said back then. "*For one thing, we've all worked too hard to have it go to our heads*". What people didn't know was that the band had an inside joke that went on for a few years; the guys invented a "Prima" award! Once a year they would give the "prize" to that Journey member who was acting like "*the biggest Prima Donna*". Steve was the one who would get it almost every year, though it was hard to believe that this nice and shy guy could ever show off! Steve was honest about that: "*The only time I really show off is onstage; that's what the audience wants and I enjoy it too*", then he added: "*The only way I know how, is to give all I got in that limited stage area. I try to generate enthusiasm and the feeling that I'm trying to talk to them; I'm this vocalist running around all over the place. Maybe if I stood still in one spot I'd die of nerves.*"

What was impossible to put a stop to, though, was the envy he was getting and some journalists at the time would make offensive remarks about

Steve. He admitted back then that he avoided the press for a couple of years and stopped reading the reviews. But the rest of the band didn't: " *The other guys in Journey would go 'Hey, Perry, look what they're calling you now', and I just didn't wanna know."* Steve wasn't troubled by the bad press, it was just that sometimes journalists would get very personal and brutal in the way they would use words and Steve just wasn't interested in reading slanderous things – he knew that ultimately the people in the audience were the ones entitled to set a verdict on him as a vocalist. And the people adored him.

Being recognized everytime he'd walk out of his door, Steve was beginning to feel the burden of fame. When he was asked about the way stardom affected him, he confessed that it was a nice thing but it didn't changed him that much: *"When you're recognized on the street, and you can't sit in a restaurant without somebody asking for an autograph, your life is changed. I've kept my perspectives in order, and the music is still the most important thing to me."*

Because he was always into the spotlight, it was no wonder why most of the criticism was aimed at him. Steve's every word was analyzed, his performances were meticulously examined and his every move was commented. But overall, as a celebrity, he didn't have what was supposed to be a reckless attitude, although he remembers a few episodes close to that definition*." If you're wondering if we've destroyed a Holiday Inn, well, sometimes it happens! One time Gregg Rolie and I went out and bought twenty-five extension cords. We figured that the extension cords were long enough to reach from our room to the first floor. We took a color television, we plugged it in and we tossed it into the pool! It was a wonderful sight!"*

Despite the general view, Steve was a humble guy and didn't consider himself a big star*." I think of myself as an entertainer – I'd rather be an entertainer. I was born to do what I'm doing -- it's like I'm fulfilling my destiny every time I get up on stage. The energy, the lights, the volume, and the people -- it's truly magic".*

In that era, Mike Hausmann was Journey's photographer and was one of the few people that had the chance to witness the band's performances from a close point of view. His pictures of the band and of Steve were seen all around the world in all the magazines and all the Journey promotions. He remembers how Steve Perry was on stage:*" He was a good dancer. Steve was a great performer and I never seen him even be a klutz ever. He would jump off stuff and land on his feet like a cat."* Although Mike was there at every concert he'd still be impressed everytime he would see the band in a live situation:*" I obviously was very close and I saw more that other people see and I never saw a bad show. Never saw a show where they weren't happy with their performance or anything. They were always just very professional and top notch."* But the show that impressed him the most was the one from 1980 at the LA Coliseum. The memories are still fresh:*" One of the biggest thrills was the L.A. Coliseum show that I did, it was almost eighty-five thousand people. If you can imagine an outdoor concert in a place where they held the Super Bowl at, that size of place, not only were all the seats filled but the playing field also was wall to wall people. It was just overwhelming to see that many people. When I was with them, that was one of the biggest shows they have done so far and it was multiple bands, there was Black Sabbath, Cheap Trick, and Blue Oyster Cult...that big of a outdoor event. You could feel it, everybody knew that this was big, everybody just had goose bumps, it was just massive. There were so many people and to hear that kind of crowd come alive during a special moment in a song or something was just, you know, it was just hard to describe".*

Mike Hausmann shared an amazing story about how Steve's mesmerizing voice would affect people. It was an impressive moment which spoke volumes about the unique connection between Steve and his fans. *"This friend of mine had a little sister that was suppose to go to a Journey concert and it was one of the shows I was shooting and she came down with like a hundred and three fever! Two days before the show they put her in intensive care in the hospital and they couldn't figure out what was wrong. She went into a coma for about 12 hours and luckily came out of it. The first thing out of her mouth was 'I'm not going to get to go to the Journey concert am I?' Her brother told me this story and I took one of my Steve Perry's pictures to the concert the next night and I asked Steve to sign it like 'Get well soon.' With the girl's name on it from Steve Perry and 'hope you make it to the next show' and it went on and on. Steve wrote this whole thing to her and the next day I went with her brother to the hospital to visit her after the show and I told her 'I said hey I am sorry that you didn't make it but I got a present for you' and I gave her this present that was the picture of Steve Perry and it was signed to her and it said 'Get Well Soon' and this girl was out of the hospital the next day and the doctors could believe it and she was so excited it just lifted her up so much that she was cured almost! Everybody thought it was a miracle and the whole family still remembers the story. Steve had the power to heal."*

*

At the beginning of November 1980, Steve was getting ready to do another album with Journey. They all thought about a name and finally they decided that "Departure" would fit with their plans as they were going to do some musical changes, departing from some of their roots and keeping some. This time Journey hired Kevin Elson to produce the new material, along with Geoff Workman.

In the recording rooms of the Automatt Studios in San Francisco nineteen new songs were ready to be shaped into timeless musical gems. They started working together, recording and deciding for the best tracks that would end up on the album. Steve was completely focused on his performance and he would spend up to four full hours daily rehearsing and warming up in the studio. Besides getting his voice in a recording quality shape, Steve was paying special attention to the meaning of his music and he was always looking for simple ways to express himself especially with lyrics because he believed in direct messages. *"I don't want to make people get too deep with what I'm trying to say"*, he said, *"Sure, I have some tunes where it takes a couple of times before you listen to it and kind of get what I meant."*

"Precious Time", one of the best songs on "Departure", was some sort of a revelation to Steve: *"I realized that time is really of the essence. It touched me and I went 'Hey now. Now before it's too late'. There's a definite message in 'Precious Time'. You've really got to hear the lyrics to get the point."* Yet, the highlight of the album was "Anyway You Want It" and it became later one of the most air-played songs of all times. This was a tune that Steve wrote with Neal Schon in one of their previous tours, while traveling in the bus, and then they finished it and recorded it for "Departure". Finally, in the Automatt Studios, Journey taped fourteen songs but only the best eleven of them eventually made it to the album. Steve stated in an interview at the time: *"For 'Departure' I sang live vocals while they were cutting basics, and I ended up keeping 90% of them. There are hardly any overdubs on this album. For example, there was one song on 'Evolution' where I did 32 vocal tracks!"*

In a short while after its release, "Departure" was topping the charts and reached triple platinum status. The release was immediately followed by a massive tour which kicked off in San Francisco and it was carefully supervised by Herbie Herbert and a numerous staff. Journey was now a huge enterprise, a music factory that was producing not only hits but also fame, fortune and worldwide interest.

"As a seed is planted so a tree shall grow" – these are the words written inside the cover of the "Departure" LP.A mysterious promise that was going to be fulfilled beyond any expectations.

*

Starting the 80s, Steve's life was changing more and more. His unmistakable voice was constantly heard throughout the FM stations across America, he was frequently interviewed, his pictures and statements were in all the rock music magazines of the time and then he was often seen on television. Besides that, he had to get used with the huge media hype he was getting on tours – all these things started affecting his privacy and his personal comfort very much. At one point he was involved in a scary situation that happened right after he finished a concert when a bunch of unruly fans waited for him to get outside the venue then literally attacked him by tearing up his shirt and pulling out his hair! Steve confessed he was scared to death and he thought he won't get out of there alive, but somehow it all ended before anything worse could've happened; Steve stated later with a touch of humor: *"Sometimes female fans can be more aggressive then men in a singles bar."*

As a consequence of this exposure, Steve began to seek hiding places where he could stay away from the limelight and recharge. Having a house of his own was a new concept for Steve because before that moment he didn't consider buying a place to live in when he was getting off tour. In one of his interviews at the time he confessed: *"It was like why have a house, you know, I wasn't even there. I just decided I'd park my car down at my parents' house, grab my suitcase and be gone. I had no possessions, nothing to really warrant having a home."* But he reconsidered and he found his safe crib in a beautiful home in Sausalito, near San Francisco, a quiet place facing the blue waters and the hills of the North Bay. *" The reason it's really special to me it's that it's my first real place after all this time on the road."* Steve's favorite recreation spot was his own living room where he could enjoy some good music and even though people wouldn't imagine that a rock star could do normal things, yet Steve was living a calm life off stage, enjoying even spending time in the kitchen cooking vegetarian meals or having the best time working around the house. On the other hand, these breaks never lasted too long because Journey was a force on the move; besides that Steve was a restless man and the road was a good place for him to get rid of all that energy. He would say: *" Sometimes I get mad at it because it takes up so much of my life, but I could never live without it. I'm a very hyper person really. That's just my personality. If I didn't have this band as some kind of release, I'd probably go nuts!"*

1980 was a highly prolific year for Steve and the band. Besides the recordings and the touring, Journey got an invitation to work on a very special project. Japan's most famous fashion designer, Kenzo Takada was making a fantasy film called "Dream After Dream" and he was searching for an American rock band that could write a specific kind of soundtrack for his movie. CBS/Sony's Japanese vice-president, Hiroshi Kani, called Neal Schon while he was doing a short promotional guitar tour in Japan and presented him Kenzo's plans. One thing led to another and finally Journey's manager, Herbie Herbert sent to Japan one of the songs that didn't made it on the "Departure" album:"Little Girl". Takada was overwhelmed by the beauty of this song and by Steve's first-class voice. That's how they settled a deal which led to one of the most fascinating musical projects that Journey ever put together. It was a great undertaking but they were willing to do it and get the best out of it.

In October 1980, after the band finished the hard six-month Departure Tour which ended in Japan with five sold-out shows in Tokyo and Osaka, Journey entered the highly advanced Shinonomachi Studios in Tokyo and in only two weeks they completed the entire project which was mostly instrumental, but three of the songs had amazing vocal parts recorded by Steve in a special way that was different from what he had done before. In front of a huge movie screen Steve had to key in the motion picture's atmosphere and he admits it was of the most captivating experiences: *"We did some crazy things with sound effects, but there are actual songs as well. It's sort of an eerie film, also. It's really a good album."*

"Dream After Dream" became one of the most wanted Journey LPs because of the band's unusual musical approach but also because it was released only in Japan.

To this day, Steve has fond memories of the times he spent in Japan, not only of the loyal Journey fan base that existed there, but also for the enjoyable off stage moments. He recalled his favorite way of spending his leisure time:*" There is a shopping area in Kyoto, it's underground and it's unbelievable! I remember the first time I saw it was just ridiculous – it would go on for miles and I could see it disappearing into the distance... I've never seen nothing like that in my life. I used to go there all the time and shop and buy all kinds of things, walk and walk for miles."* Being a lover of spicy foods, Steve was savoring Japan's exotic offers as well: *"I like Wasabi! I poured it on everything! It's good but it makes my voice sound hoarse because it irritates it."*

With "Dream After Dream" completed, Steve got home from Japan and was ready to get back to the Journey timetable which meant rehearsing, writing songs and preparing for the next studio album. Meanwhile, on the 8th of January 1981 another Journey LP was released and this one was destined to become one of the best ones in the band's career:" Captured".

Sixteen songs were recorded live all through March and April 1980, during the Departure World Tour; three songs from Montreal, Canada, two from the Tokyo concert in Japan and the others from a show in Detroit, Michigan. Those were sixteen flawless renditions of the biggest Journey hits at that time. The energy and the state-of-the-art performance made this album unequaled through time. "Captured" had a special studio addition: a song previously written by Steve called "The Party Is Over" which was recorded at Fantasy Studios in California. Steve still has in mind the memory of how this song was born. He was in Detroit playing around with a bass guitar backstage at Cobo Hall when he came up with this song. He went on stage and played it with the band at sound check and it was finished that day. The song ended up being the perfect closing moment for the "Captured" breathtaking sound trip.

By the time Journey ended their 1980 tour, shocking news hit the rock community: Bon Scott, the singer of AC/DC had lost his life. He was a good friend of all the Journey members so they decided to dedicate "Captured" to the memory of Bon Scott. Steve had a special admiration for Bon Scott. He remembers being in Texas and having AC/CD opening the show for Journey. Steve recalls coming around the stage to warm up before his performance; AC/DC were towards the end of their show and Steve was watching them from the wings. He was very impressed. *"It was the most amazing live show. Those guys were great and they really helped us to become a better band. From that point on I was a huge AC/DC, Bon Scott fan."*

Journey's first live album confirmed once more that Steve was a magnificent artist, able to set a new vocal standard for concert performances. Finally, he was on the mountaintop and the sky was the limit. At that point Steve had already won twice the Best Male Vocalist award at the Bay Area Music Awards in 1980 and 1981.

It was the beginning of 1981 when Journey was getting ready for the month of March when they would begin full-scale rehearsals for their new studio album. But something changed. Gregg Rolie, Journey's keyboard player, was getting tired of the hectic life on the road and while the band was touring in Germany he announced his band mates that when they would get back in the U.S. he was intending to retire, have a family and focus on his personal life. Steve explained to the press of the time what led to Rolie's decision: *"He'd been talking for a long time about how he doesn't like the road. It can be pretty grueling. When you're home only two or three months out of a year, and only three or four weeks of that time is actually to yourself because the rest is back to work in the studio or rehearsing, it can get to you."* Gregg Rolie was a very special friend to Steve as they had shared many fine moments together. In one of his latest interviews, Steve evoked his times with Gregg:*" In the very beginning I have to say that Gregg Rolie was the guy who took me under his wing. I had nowhere to stay in the bay area and he put me in a downstairs bedroom of his house. He was a really supportive guy and really was positively behind the idea of me being in the band."*

Before leaving the band, Rolie pointed out a replacement for him: Jonathan Cain. He knew Journey needed a good keyboard player to help them go on with their next album. Cain, who was playing at the time with a group called "The Babys", was asked to join Journey and he accepted.

From that moment on something magic happened.

On The Top Of The World

"It was a rainy day one time in San Francisco...I had this idea for a song, so I called Jonathan and I went up to his house...We started working on the tune, it started developing...The idea was about the one that had got away, the one you wish you still had...And the rain kept coming down...and I was wondering... who's crying now?"*

September 1981, Alpine Valley Amphitheater, Wisconsin: Steve is on stage next to Jonathan Cain's big red piano and his voice gets emotional as he tells the story of this song. From time to time he stops and listens to the velvety sound of Jon's piano. In private, Jonathan called it *"a somebody done something wrong song"*. Steve came up with this melody one time when he was driving his car through the San Joaquin Valley and he was singing into a cassette recorder. Now he was in front of this huge audience remembering the way it all came together...The crowd goes wild as he sings the opening lines of "Who's Crying Now".

That was the first single from the newest album of the band that had been released just a few months back in that year of 1981:" Escape". Steve loved that song and really believed it its powerful message. But he and Jonathan had to fight for this song's quality, because sometimes the people who were not involved in the writing process wouldn't understand the value of the music alone. In one of his latest interviews, Steve recalled how things went then:" *'Who's Crying Now' was intentionally recorded and arranged so that the solo was at the end. The record label came to us and said 'as soon as the solo starts you'll have to fade it or radio won't play it.' I said ' well, radio can fade out and go onto the news. I don't care, but we're not going to cut the solo.' I said 'look – Neal played the most beautiful solo on this thing. It's simple, heartfelt and feels timeless; the melodics are timeless and I do not want to kill that solo'. So, I fought for it, the song became a hit and the stations never pulled out of the solo."* "Who's crying now" became an ageless hit and one of the most recognizable classic Journey songs. Neal Schon's brilliant solo was never faded and even more: today no one could imagine that song without that solo all the way! Steve's musical insight was, like always, picture perfect.

Journey was now ready to get on the top of the world.

*

The magic was there, it was almost tangible. The chemistry was even more compelling and Steve was having now a new ally in his efforts to reveal the quintessence of his feelings in the songs. Jonathan Cain was inspiring him and together they'd start writing some amazing tunes that would change not only Journey's sound but the very sound of rock music as it was known. Before actually recording "Escape", there were a lot of ideas. There were words telling stories about personal experiences, there were beautiful guitar lines and sensual piano notes, there was a voice that would blend brilliantly with the music and put a heart in each song…it was really powerful. Steve confesses that the best songs were written on the road, during the lengthy tours when he was living in a special environment. He would carry a cassette player with him all the time and record every single musical line that would come into his mind. Before every show Steve was experiencing the unique feeling of being able to walk into a big Coliseum with no people in it and get inspirational because of the nice echo that these places had; he would get ideas just by listening to the sounds that were generated in there. He admitted: *"I think there was a point in the band during Escape where it turned such a corner and it just started coming so fast."*

Now, after more than twenty years after it was brought to the world, "Escape" is a milestone of the 20th century's music. Not long ago, Steve tried to explain the secret behind the massive success of the "Escape" album:*" I think one of the reasons is because there was a certain type of acoustic texture. I'm talking specifically of the introduction of Jonathan Cain when we had keyboard and voice singing and the acoustics ,then all of a sudden Neal's electric would come in. We choreographed and arranged in such a way that it was a new texture for us. I think that had a lot to do with the palatability of the album."*

But back then they didn't even dream about the impact that "Escape" will have and they were doing everything only by using their deep artistic instincts. Song by song, the album was getting in shape and Steve remembers the exact moment when things started to change. It was the day Jon Cain came to his house and he played a song for Steve: *"I asked him what that was and he said, "This is just a song that I started. I played it for my wife and I played it for John Waite but he said it was too syrupy".* But Steve loved it so much, he wanted to finish it then and there. He remembers: *"That particular one kind of wrote itself in one afternoon. It went that quick."*

"Open Arms", one of the greatest power-ballads in AOR's history, was ready to reach millions of people, and somehow Steve and Jon realized it was different from everything Journey has done before. First they had to go and play the song for the rest of the group. *"They were opposed to the ballad"*, remembers Steve. It was hard to convince a hard rocking guitarist like Neal Schon to embrace such a song and he even said he didn't understood what his role could be in a ballad like that one; then he called it a *"Marry Poppins kinda song"*. There were endless discussions on whether "Open Arms" should be on the new album and at one point the song was almost dumped. But finally Steve decided it was best to record it and he remembers how he had to sing in the recording booth under the sarcastic eyes of Neal Schon who still didn't believe in the song at that time. After a few attempts to finish the song, Steve stopped and said he will record "Open Arms" only if Neal gets out of the studio... which he did. Steve started over the recording and as he got further into the song, his voice became more emotional and warmhearted .He really believed in the meaning of that song. *"There is one line in 'Open Arms' that I always wanted to be a certain way. The line "wanting you near" – I just wanted that line to go up and soar. I wanted it to be heartfelt."*

Later that year, when Journey went on the "Escape' Tour and played the song for the first time to the people in the audience, all doubts melted away. "Open Arms" became a signature song for Journey and many years after, Steve recaptured the reaction of the crowd when they played it live on stage:*" The place went crazy! Just nuts! I looked over at Neal and he was stunned. We did two encores then we got backstage... I'm walking back there and all of a sudden Neal's going:' Man, that song kicked a**!' And I looked at him and I wanted to kill him."*

*

In the spring of 1981, the recordings for "Escape" were going just great. The production was handled by Kevin Elson who was also the band's sound engineer during the tours. Elson knew this was a special project and he was looking for a different recording feeling: *"There is a spark that we are trying to capture on vinyl that exists in the live Journey show"*, he said. Steve was in an excellent vocal shape and the songs were coming together like never before. Jonathan Cain recalled how smoothly everything went:*" Steve probably sang the 'Mother, Father' vocal in two takes. Done. It seemed like the whole band could just get up and fly away."*

Another highpoint of the album was this song called "Don't Stop Believing" that was sketched during the rehearsal session at the bands Oakland warehouse. It started with a guitar line then Steve and Jonathan took over by adding a certain touch to the song that made it sound glorious. Steve remembers exactly how the idea of the lyrics was born:*" We were in Detroit and I was at the hotel downtown, and we'd finish the show, I 'm not sleepy because I'm jacked from the show and I'm looking down, and the city streets are all quiet, but there's all these people on the streets, on the corner, and these streetlights, and I'm thinking, man, it's unbelievable, people just creeping late at night; Jonathan and I got together and started working on this, and when we started working on the lyrics, that moment came to mind and I think I discussed it with Jonathan."*

"Don't Stop Believing" became almost like a rock anthem for the 80s generation and its uplifting tempo as well as its message never ceased to inspire people all around the world.

The "Escape" album sold over forty million copies worldwide and it turned out to be one of the best sold rock albums of all times. In 1981, the LP spent seven weeks in a row at the number one position in the US charts. More so, "Escape" is considered to this day a point of reference in the history of American adult oriented rock music.

With all this good music they were delivering, their success grew more and more each day. The five musicians of Journey were so famous that they even had their own video game which was an absolute premiere. In 1982, Journey and Data Age Inc. released a game for the Atari 2600 making Journey the first rock band to enter into the video game industry! The main design of the game was about getting all five members from the concert stage to their Scarab Escape Vehicle. The player had to "guide" the Journeymen all the way through the masses of Love-Crazed Groupies and other backstage obstacles, while a computerized version of "Don't Stop Believing" was playing in the background. The game was a success and it was a definite must have in the 80s!

Despite their massive triumph, the band had to deal with unwarranted criticism coming from jealous voices that would say Journey was a formulaic band. Steve defended their beliefs explaining that Journey never created anything that was calculated or conventional as for them the music was all about feelings: *"The band truly follows its heart. Nobody ever thought of doing power ballads before we came up with it. With Neal Schon on guitar we had the ability to do that. The critics could never see that."* Even though reviewers were attacking Steve as well, he was protecting the Journey concept whenever he was approached with questions about his thoughts about the group's success : *"In Journey you have five professional strong independent players and they are virtuosos in their own right.(...) When you're not successful people just burn you to the ground, you know... In the beginning, when Journey didn't do well, they would say ,and I quote them, "diffused energy, diffused direction, lack of cohesiveness no focal point, nothing interesting, frenzy guitar playing", all this stuff...Now, the same critics are saying we are commercial. The point is the people are the ones that decide."* But no matter what the press was saying and despite the cruel reviews they were getting sometimes, Journey was out there for those who believed in true music and nothing could stop them from carrying out their mission.

After attending the Bay Area Music Awards in March of 1981,Steve was ready again for heavy touring .He left behind the comfort of his home and got geared up for the Great Escape World Tour which began in June with three remarkable concerts at the Calaveras County Fairgrounds where the band finally introduced their new member, Jonathan Cain.

One of the major highlights of the new tour was the fantastic show at the Rose Bowl in Pasadena on July 2nd in front of almost one hundred thousand people! This incredible rock marathon of the bands at the Fourth Of July Weekend Festival went on for hours under the hot California summer sun, but everyone from the bands to the people in the crowd were having a blast! That day Blue Oyster Cult, Triumph and Aldo Nova were the opening acts and for the grand finale, Journey went up on stage and rocked the night in front of an ecstatic audience. For many years to come, a lot of people remembered that show and named it on of the best ones of all times.

Starting the 27th of July, Journey took the Escape circuit out to Japan for a few weeks, followed by a comeback to Canada. Then starting August 22nd they came to rock the US again performing night after night in front of millions of people who were receiving Journey's new music with even more enthusiasm as before. The "Escape" album was the absolute number one record in the US right after its release on the 1st of July, and it was riding the highest wave all around the world. By September 1981, the record went Gold and then Platinum on the same day!

The press, the critics and the entire media was following Journey's break out to the top and soon enough they were approached by the newest TV channel at the time: Music Television. They were willing to capture some of Journey's shows on tape and broadcast them full length. The television industry concepts were evolving and MTV was definitely a revolutionary brainchild in the mass-media of the era. The band's management went on with the idea, but Steve was pretty nervous about that. He would be put in a video recording situation that was not always pleasing to him, but he couldn't do anything but get used to the fact that this was a new media movement and

Journey was in it. That's how the show performed and filmed by MTV on the 6th of November 1981 at the Houston Summit in Texas, was set to remain one of the high points of all time live concerts. Twenty-four years later, in 2005, Steve decided to bring that performance back to life on a DVD. Using the newest studio technology and the contribution of some of the best people in the business, the Houston Summit concert turned into an everlasting masterpiece. Without any doubt, the show stood the test of time and it's considered one of the most brilliant Journey performances ever. While working on the production of this DVD, Steve's memories of those times were still fresh as he recalled the event in a recent interview: *"To be perfectly honest with you, I was always apprehensive when it came to having recording trucks in the parking lot and cameras on stage.(...) It was difficult because you would have to worry about cameramen in front of you or behind you"*. Back then, Steve had arguments with the management about the situation, but eventually the idea turned out to be the best: *"Management won the battle and they were right. This concert did need to be recorded and I am so glad that it was because I had no idea it was that good."*

Looking back on his performance at the Houston Summit concert, Steve had a revelation about his own self: *"This young kid up there on that stage believed in what he believed in and damned if it wasn't pretty good and I got emotional about it. I just felt vindicated. I really felt vindicated for my beliefs and my faith and my tenacity that I got such a bad rep for... it's just that I was NOT going to lay down."*

All the way through the 1981 Escape Tour, people were completely spellbound by Steve's impeccable live vocal skills and they would often state that he sounded even better live on stage than in the studio. Steve confessed back then that nothing in the world could have matched his joy when he was singing live. He was absolutely thrilled by their new album: *"I do think Escape comes closer to capturing our live sound than any of our previous studio albums. I think, unquestionably, it's the best studio album we've ever done."*

At one point during the tour, Journey had to face a demanding situation - a certain concert in Philadelphia at the JFK Stadium. That night, they accepted again to be the opening act for a veteran band: The Rolling Stones. Steve was ready to get up on stage to do his best and was confident both in his capabilities and Journey's music. They were only given forty-five minutes to play and Steve was perfectly aware that the Stones' fans were not Journey's fans. But as soon as he walked out there and started singing, the battle was won: Steve captivated all those people with his beautiful voice and in just a few minutes the audience was under the spell of the music. Jonathan Cain was excited but sort of amused, too, as he stated in an interview at the time: *"It was the thrill of a lifetime in one respect! We had the best selling album in the country at the moment, but yet we were there showing a ninety thousand people that we were willing to be an opening act! They were yelling that Steve Perry couldn't sing like Mick Jagger! Hopefully not: Steve Perry is a trained vocalist.*" Jon Cain was new in the band and didn't had the chance to witness the previous encounter between Journey and The Rolling Stones which happened before - it was that one show during the Infinity Tour in July of 1978 in Chicago at the Soldiers Field stadium where they had to face an all Rolling Stone audience. But this time, in Philadelphia, the JFK arena was packed with Journey supporters.

One year later, after topping the charts with "Escape" and successfully touring the world from the US to Japan and back, after being downright loved by the press, then criticized by envious voices, then adored and loved by the fans, the band needed to take a break. Steve could finally find some peace of mind and took some time to meditate on Journey's success: *" We've worked damn hard to get where we are today"*, Steve said, *"The type of music that we do is rather complex at times and it can be difficult to write and record. The only thing that really concerns us is making the best music we can. "*

Yet, a long vacation was not Journey's thing, so pretty soon the band decided to regroup and think about the next album. Meanwhile, almost without noticing, Journey was becoming a business enterprise that would set new standards in the industry. The year they were all looking forward to was 1983.

A New Frontier

"*At the JFK Stadium* in *Philadelphia, ninety thousand people gathered to welcome a band of traveling musicians. The band they honor is named Journey.*"

That is how "Frontiers & Beyond" begins. A one hour and a half filmed documentary about the far-reaching mission the most beloved rock band of America was fulfilling within each day of their new tour. With an impressive style, John Facenda, NFL's well-known figure, narrated the story of Journey. "Frontiers & Beyond" had a detailed insight on the way the Journey machinery worked on tour and also a view on each band member as well as on the crew members. Pat Morrow, Journey's road manager at the time said: *"Consistency is the best thing in this business. There are thirty three people that work with me for Journey and we are all obsessed with Journey's success; they want a better performance every night .I've never seen anyone as self-critical as this band. Everyone is totally implied."* It was for the first time when the public could take a look behind the stage lights and behind Steve's public image. "Frontiers & Beyond" ended with one of the most impressive Journey concerts captured on tape by fourteen professional cameras on the 4th of June 1983.

After the movie was released, everyone realized that Journey was not only a trained, well-organized band but it truly was the hardest working bunch of musicians in the industry.

In January 1983 the "Frontiers" album was released and soon it reached the highest selling figures. But it was more than just the music – Journey was a powerful business, put together by a staff of experts. Everything was set up to bring out the best in front of the people who were attending Journey's concerts. This was the beginning of a new era in rock music as well. The Frontiers Tour would provide new standards for all the rock artists to come. For the first time in the live acts' records, the concert technology would surpass anything it was done until that moment. Journey had a custom made stage, a computerized lighting system and a mind-boggling innovation: huge twenty foot video screens and five professional TV cameras that were capturing and displaying on the big screens all the action on the stage and the members of the band while performing; this new approach made it possible for every spectator to feel like they were up in the front rows.

This revolutionary idea came around one day when Steve had a talk with the band members and the management about the huge venues where they were going to perform. Steve was always interested in having the closest connection possible with the people in the audience; his main concern now was that not everyone out there would see the band up-close as the huge arenas kept people in the back rows away from all the stage action. So he said it would be fantastic if, as an alternative, they would bring the band closer to those people through video screens! The idea was brilliant, but there was a problem: no one had done that before in a concert situation so they didn't even knew if such a technology existed! Manager Herbie Herbert decided to look for possibilities. He was so determined to make it happen he said that if there's no such thing as a huge screen for a concert venue they will create one! In a short while, they put together all the logistic and the equipment to complete this ground-breaking project. It was a huge, revolutionary step that would put Journey into the league of the pioneers and trend-setters. Later, every major rock group from America wanted to use that kind of stage set-up. From that moment Journey changed the live act concept forever.

Now the band was ready to get on the road again and this time every step of the Frontiers Tour was going to be witnessed by a crew of producers from NFL Films. The band's schedule was impressive: *"The Journey 'Frontiers' Tour will cover seventy-two cities and provide a hundred and ten concerts for over two million people.(...)Criss-crossing the country in seven cockpit trailers and three buses, towing the portable pieces of state-of-the-art rock and roll, this journey will take them to new frontiers and beyond."*

But as always, before any tour it was the creation: the music for the new album. At the end of 1982, the band started working on the "Frontiers" LP which was supposed to have a new sound. Steve and the band wanted to move into uncharted musical territories and find new ways of expressing their creative vision. The songwriting began six months earlier, while they were still on the road. "Separate Ways", the opening song on the new album, was put together in a single afternoon by Steve and Jon Cain somewhere in New York with the help of Jonathan's little Casio keyboard. Steve brought into play his strong Motown roots and that added a special feeling and a strong haunting rhythm to it. At that time they didn't plan to make this a song for a new album but they kept it because it was too good to be wasted. The idea of the song came from the personal problems that some of the band members were having at the time. With Neal Schon and Ross Valory going through heartbreaking divorces, Steve and Jon thought there should be a way to find something positive out of such circumstances. Steve said: *"There's got to be a more soulful way of looking at things."*

At the time Steve often visited Jon at his house where he had a mini-studio and they would sketch songs together. That's how one day, Jonathan played this special piano line to Steve. He loved the tune and he worked on it both on the sound and lyrics. Jon said:*" Steve could magically weave a melody over anything I could play"* .That's how "Send Her My Love" was born, a song that would become one of Steve's all time favorites." *This song is cinematic",* he said later,*" it's got some kind of visuals to it, a little more than most. It's in the sound of the instruments, the feel of the drums, the character of the voice and the echoes".*

Although "Frontiers" was built up to make a fresh musical statement, the band wouldn't give up their sensitivity as they strongly believed in the power of their ballads. That`s why Jon Cain wrote "Faithfully" which was a view over a musician's life on tour and how it was affecting the lives of all the others involved. Steve added a heart melting vocal line to this track that became one the greatest hits not only in Journey's career, but in AOR`s history. This amazing song came together with a special video; the band made a short film right when they were on the road, capturing the image of the hard touring band they were and showing all of them in their off-stage environment: in the buses during the traveling from city to city, at the sound checks or backstage. This video turned into a sort of a classic short Journey movie.

With the new album, Steve's songwriting abilities were getting more and more intense and he definitely added a unique quality to each and every new song on the record. One of the things he wanted to change on this new album was his singing manner. He knew that it would be a daring move but he felt it was a good time to explore his vast vocal range. For this, Steve somewhat moved away from his famous singing style and dropped a bit the high ranges, although on some songs he still used his full strength, high-pitched sound. With this amend, Steve's voice gained even more emotion than before, but, to his surprise, some people misunderstood the change of style. Rumors started circulating and they were all saying that the reason for Steve's lower voice must've been a hidden disease like throat cancer or some developing vocal damage that he wanted to conceal. Of course, nothing of that was true and at the beginning he wanted to fight all those malicious stories. Eventually he gave up – he wasn't going to waste precious time trying to stop a rumor mill gone wild. Back then Steve made a few statements in order to respond to the questions about the change of his vocal fashion: *"It was a very conscious decision on my part. I think that the first thing that someone can get tired of in a band is the vocals. If you don't try to change a bit that sound can get tiring; I was anxious to try and use my lower range more. I have greater strength in my overall presentation."* Then he added jokingly: *"I find that the longer we tour the higher my voice gets. I know that by the end of the last tour we were attracting small animals backstage because I was hitting notes that only they could hear!"*

In November 1982, Steve and the band started rehearsing for the new LP somewhere in a Bay area warehouse .The place was equipped with everything they needed and it was so big that they could even rehearse their live show. Preparations took a couple of weeks, the already existing songs were polished, new ones were written right there, every track was carefully chosen and arranged, but they've left enough room for ad-libbing.

Soon after that, the recording session started at Fantasy Studios in Berkley and Journey hired Mike Stone and Kevin Elson to handle the production part for the "Frontiers" album. It was an intense recording session, mostly because it was performed live just like in a concert situation. Steve's voice was in perfect shape and there wasn't much to revise after he finished putting his vocals on the tracks.

When the record was almost done, Michael Dilbeck, Journey's longtime A&R man, took a last minute decision and replaced two songs: he put "Back Talk" and "Troubled Child" in, and took out "Ask the Lonely" and "Only the Young".With this new track list, the brand new album was released on the 19th of February 1983 and in a short while it sold over five million copies.

The Frontiers Tour was scheduled to go across America for six months - the circuit started off on the 23rd of March in Seattle then it was planned to cover all the major venues from Hawaii to New York. One of the many stops in California was in Fresno, a place where Steve had lived for many years – it was like returning home and singing for old friends. On July 31st, Journey had a sold-out show in Fresno, and Steve wanted to make this moment one to remember. He and the band decided this was going to be a benefit concert for the Valley Children's Hospital and the next day the band handed over a giant check for fifty thousand dollars! Journey was more than just music – it was about love and compassion, too; this was one of the many acts of kindness that the band members would do over the years.

The Frontiers Tour ended on September 7, 1983 with five sold-out shows at Blaisedale Coliseum in Honolulu, Hawaii, where, despite of the road exhaustion, Steve was keeping up his high standard performance. Everyone remembers to this day the outstanding concerts and Steve's staggering vocal charisma; he was wearing his heart on his sleeve and people were responding with tremendous love. In fact, Steve's devotion for the fans was one the most important reasons that kept him going. His happiness of being up there on stage was evident and people remembered the moment he said to the Hawaiian audience: *"What better place in the world to end a tour then here in paradise!"* It was a triumph. In 1983 a Gallup Poll named

Journey the most popular group of the year. Statistics showed that the Frontiers Tour was attended by almost two million people who paid a total of twenty-seven million dollars to see their favorite musicians performing live. But behind the success and the recognition, this huge undertaking came with a price for every band member as well as the crew. Looking back on those days, Steve became aware of the clear picture. The touring was rough, none of them were getting enough rest, they were in a different place every single day and all of this started taking its toll on everyone. *"At that point we had worked so hard and I think we were, as a group, seeing so much of each other. That's what happens in bands. In the middle of the Frontiers Tour and definitely at the end of the tour we were pretty stressed and I was burnt."*

But no matter how brutal things were, Steve was performing every night with the same passion and commitment. He was living and breathing through music. To keep things in perspective he would observe the technical crew. He noticed how dedicated the crew members were – they were sleeping very little if at all, they would be the first ones up in the morning and working hard until the show was about to begin, then after the concert was over they would tear down the stage, make sure everything is set for the road and then start all over again the next morning. It was a strenuous task for each and every one of them, but they were working with a lot of zeal and devotion. Steve was learning valuable lessons: *"It's a good reminder of the band to see that."*, he confessed, *"I particularly like to hang out with the crew. I m honest with you – in this business you can have the tendency when you're successful to get pretty puffed up, you know, it's very easy, you got so many people around you telling you how wonderful you are, how great you are and you can get yourself blown out of perspective. Just to be with the crew and see how hard they work and touch base with them keeps your feet right on the ground."*

At the end of the Frontiers Tour, after taking over the stadiums and rewarding their fans with hours of great rock music, it was time to try something else. The music television era was just about to begin.

*

At the start of the 80s, MTV was still something new and different. The young generation of the era was attracted to visuals much more than before. It was the new age of the selling image, a concept that would be embraced by many of the rock groups of that time. Journey was having a great relationship with MTV since the beginning, as the station had filmed an entire Houston Summit Journey show in 1981. The band was also involved in the station's "One Night Stand" competition in which the big prize included a special treat: three friends were flown in a Lear jet to a Journey concert!

Now the guys were ready to do their first concept videos - a new thing not only for them but for the music business as well considering that back then only a few bands had videos to their songs. However, Steve wasn't won over yet by the video notion and he was hoping that the music will still come first. A few years later he would declare:*" The imagination of the music it's where we start with a song. Sometimes the video do not follow through and changes the course of our fantasy that the song was written from. And it's very important for us as songwriters to protect that fantasy; we're trying to protect people's availability to visualize a song like they perceive it."*

Yet Journey was willing to try the new thing. They went for two of the best songs from the "Frontiers" album, "Separate Ways" and "Chain Reaction". The video production crew was taking the first creative steps and these Journey videos were a positive experience for everyone involved. Before arriving at the location, Steve spent time on the phone with Jessica Scott, the video art director, trying to explain to her the feelings conveyed in each song. From the way the ideas were coming into shape, this was going to be an interesting endeavor for the band members.

In 1983, a few days before Mardi-Gras, Journey flew out from San Francisco to New Orleans and at ten o'clock in the morning they saw the location for the first time. It was at the Louisa Street Wharf, near a blue warehouse facing the Mississippi river. They were going to start off filming the first part of "Separate Ways" and the art director's story on the song had fifty-six camera movements. That first day the shots were concentrated on the band members. Steve had to follow the director's indications and one of them was that he won't be having a microphone in his hand. That made Steve feel pretty weird:*" I feel naked without a mike"*, he said. Even though he was supposed to lip-synch the song, Steve felt he needed to get in the ambiance and he actually sang for real, with his voice powerful enough to be heard over the amplified song that was blasting from the speakers. On the other hand, a cold wind was blowing that day which made Steve run for a warm shelter between takes. As the day went by, half of the takes were done and the entire band turned out to be more confident in the final results. The second day of the shooting was located on the other side of the warehouse. Steve was already affected by the unreasonable cold weather and he caught a cold. Despite the uncomfortable feeling, he finished his part without any problems and by the end of that day the whole song was filmed.

The next evening, the producers and the band relocated in a film ...udio in New Orleans where the second video, "Chain Reaction", was going to be captured on film in an art-deco set which was built in three days. The band was determined to get out the best of the project and eventually, everything turned out to be not only fun but very creative as well. At a later date, the band went back to the same studio and shot the third video for a song off of the "Frontiers" album: "After The Fall". This one became one of the most watched Journey videos to this day. All three productions went on heavy rotation on MTV's video playlists of that that year and not only increased the number of fans but it also pushed the sales of the "Frontiers" album up to multi-platinum, proving that the visuals era had already built some solid ground to expand on.

Journey's splendid evolution into the most popular rock band of America brought them in 1983 a nomination for a Star on the Hollywood Walk of Fame Boulevard. Still, it took twenty-two years for that dream to come true, but it was worth the wait: starting January 2005, the Journey Star has its well deserved place on the Hollywood Walk of Fame as a legitimate recognition of their outstanding career and their huge contribution to Rock and Roll's history.

The Call Of The Street

Steve always knew that one day his musical roots will push him to write the songs that he'd been keeping in his heart since he was a young boy. The need of spreading his wings and exploring his inner musical self was too powerful to ignore. The time was quite right to start thinking about a solo project as the other Journey members were already having their solo efforts officially released. More so, the break they all took from heavy touring was allowing them to have some time for themselves. Steve admitted: *"I don't want to tour as much as seven or eight months' extravaganzas."*

Creativity was something that had always been Steve's second nature and this was the best time to follow his muse. A few weeks after the Frontiers Tour was done, Steve moved to Los Angeles and started working on his first solo record. As he recalled later, it was a quick and simple decision:*" I jumped in my car, drove to Los Angeles, I rented a house and wrote the songs."* Steve bears in mind the time and place when he felt he should make a decision about doing some music on his own. It was during the recordings that he'd done with Kenny Loggins, another great singer and songwriter of the 80s, who invited Steve to be his vocal guest on this album he was working on. Steve and Kenny made a great duet on "Don't Fight It" – a song that went high up in the charts and was nominated in 1984 for a Grammy for Best Rock Vocal Performance by a Duo or Group. For Steve, that wonderful feeling of creative freedom was very appealing.*" Doing that song was a fun experience"*, he said,*" I learned from Kenny that each song doesn't have to be a hit. Our attitude was if we didn't come up with something we liked, then we wouldn't record it."* Kenny Loggins was more than excited to work with Steve on the song:*"Steve is capable of hitting high notes that most of rock singers can't conceive of"*, Loggins said, *"He also has a soulful quality that makes his voice truly unique. When you hear Perry's voice on the radio, you know instantly that it's him. His vocal talent is so special that it draws attention on its own."* However, working with Kenny Loggins wasn't the only occasion that made Steve think about a musical project of his own. Earlier that year he met Dewey Bunnell the lead singer of the rock group America. Dewey and Steve were both living in Marin County and they ran into each other at a Home Depot store in the area. They became friends and the next thing was that Steve was invited to join up with the band and work on America's upcoming album for 1984 called "Perspective". They wrote a beautiful love song together called "Can't Fall Asleep To A Lullaby", and then Steve went into the studio and recorded an excellent vocal line.

Meanwhile, Steve already had some songs sketched for his solo project and he was thrilled: this was going to be his "baby", a different musical statement that he wanted to make for a long time. Immediately after arriving in Los Angeles, Steve started putting together the band that would work with him in the studio and he decided to find some rather unknown musicians to start out this project. Although they were not in the limelight, they were all extremely talented. As soon as they were contacted, they were enthusiastic about the idea of teaming up with Steve Perry. One of these musicians was drummer Larry Londin who was considered one of Motown's best drummers; Londin was well known for he had played on most of Elvis Presley's albums. Another one of them was Craig Kampf, an old friend with whom Steve had worked before in the 70s in the "Alien Project" band. *"I love to work with other people"*, Steve admitted, *" they help bring things out in myself I think."* He remembers exactly how the day when they all got together was:*" They thought I might come in the studio acting like a big-time rock star and starting ordering them around. I was the complete opposite. Once everyone sat down for a pizza and beer – my personal vices - all the tension was gone."*

Obviously, Steve and his new band had a great musical chemistry going on and in less than four weeks he wrote all the material with Randy Goodrum and John Bettis, two of his best friends who were sharing the same musical view as Steve; soon he went into a studio in Detroit and recorded ten songs under the album name of "Street Talk". The music and the lyrics had very special meaning to Steve: for example,"Captured By The Moment" talks about the tragic deaths of Steve's favorite musicians: Sam Cooke - his idol- then Jimi Hendrix, Janis Joplin any many other great musicians that left this world too early. More than that, Steve was still under the impression of Marvin Gaye's violent death that occurred on the 1st of April in that very same year of 1984 when Steve was working on his solo album. Marvin Gaye was one of his all time favorite singers. With "Captured by the Moment", he wanted to pay a tribute to those artists that he grew up with and from whom he had learned so much.

Steve was having the time of his life working on the songs, giving them the significance that he wanted them to have. He had a convincing story for every song, because he said they came from real life experiences. "Foolish Heart" was one of the most poignant tracks of the album and, as Steve explained, the source of inspiration was a sentimental dilemma: *"The felling basically was one of being confused of falling back in love again, because your heart wants to do so, but your head says 'wait a minute, you've* done that before and it doesn't feel good'. It's just that real titter totter of the head and heart conflict that I think everybody goes through." About "Running Alone", another heartfelt track from the album, Steve said: "Sometimes the fear involved when you decide to move or do something else will keep you in places you don't want to be. You have to decide that you're not afraid to lose – or running alone - then you can go ahead, go anywhere and do anything." Steve's ties to Motown and R'n'B were noticeable throughout the entire album. He explained the new approach: "There was a certain texture and guttural type of thing I did to my voice to try to achieve a different texture. Part of that was recording early in the day when my voice was still 'gruff'"

In the interviews of the time, Steve confessed that he was experiencing an "infectious feeling of freedom" ,as he named it, and more: "Freedom is an amazing feeling. Once you get it you don't want to give it up. I'm really feeling it -it's this incredible thing rushing through me". Shortly after he started working on the record, rumors kicked off, all saying that the Journey days were counted. But Steve never had any intention to leave his "cradle", all he wanted was a mere break to do what he felt like it was his own personal music. However, he knew from previous experiences that rumors could not be stopped. It was the same everytime one of the Journey members was working on individual projects, then the hearsay would stop as soon as they'd get back to the Journey projects. Anyway, Steve didn't care about the rumor mill. The only thing he wanted was to be able to do what he'd been longing for. Asked about how he felt working on such a demanding solo project, Steve admitted that success was a tricky thing. After everything he achieved with Journey he thought he would be satisfied if that was all he would ever have. He was surprised by his own reactions: "I soon found out that when you've had a taste of success you start craving more." However, he was very happy with his solo project: "'Street Talk' is the most satisfying thing that I've ever experienced because I coordinated the whole product myself. I financed the project, I booked the studio, I co-produced the records, found the musicians and wrote the material." He added later: "It takes wearing many hats for objectivity to be a producer."

When "Street Talk" was released after six months, in April 1984, the success was instant: the LP climbed the best-selling albums chart and went platinum in no time. Steve decided to dedicate his first solo record to the bass player from his first band Alien Project, Richard Michaels, who died in a car crash and also to Steve Potter, who died in a similar car accident. Potter was a musician who played with Steve in the same high school band. The liner notes of "Street Talk" were equally covering happiness and sadness – Steve expressed a lot of his personal feelings both through music and words. "Oh, Sherrie", the first single of the album, rocketed the Top Ten charts as fast as lightning. This song was written for his girlfriend at the time and it was put together in just one night in a hotel room where Steve and two of his Street Talk musicians, Bill Cuomo and Craig Krampf started out a song-writing session from midnight to five in the morning: *" We had no lyrics, no nothing"*, Steve remembered, *" Just a bunch of mumbles on tape, certain vowel sounds and things, but that sort of started the whole idea. And next thing I know the song was almost finished and it was such a personal song. I really needed someone with a good lyric insight like Randy Goodrum had and he helped me finish the lyrics on it."*

"Foolish Heart" and "Strung Out" were the other two singles that topped the charts and the radio stations all over America were playing all these songs in heavy rotation. Steve was absolutely ecstatic about the fact that people loved his creations. That's all he ever wanted. He was enjoying his success so much sometimes he'd do funny things: *"When I drive down the street and I hear my song on the radio, I want to tell the person in the next car to listen to me on the radio! I did that once and the person thought I was nuts! But I had a smile on my face for the rest of the ride!"*

Although his music was conquering the radio, Steve was aware that those were the 80s and the music videos were getting more and more significant. The music channels were already a powerful medium for worldwide exposure. He decided to make videos for all the three singles off of "Street Talk", but he was determined to do them his own way. He still wasn't a video enthusiast, at least not in the video concepts department so he thought it would be a good chance to express his own opinions through the image. The videos for "Oh, Sherrie" and "Strung Out" turned out to be satirical, sarcastic punches toward the video music industry at the time. Both productions were directed by Jack Cole and had a similar outset and they even shared the same funny character: a dreadful woman by the name of "Sheila". Steve explained the idea: *"Sheila is a character who's like the publicist from the record company who always says 'Dahling, you're wundaful, wundaful' and tells you what you want to hear all the time – a little on the obnoxious side!"* As for the message of his music and the meaning of videos in general, Steve was seeing things in a different way than the vast majority at the time and he wasn't going to walk the same pathways as everybody else. He remembers how things went back in the days: *" What was hard first of all was finding a director; most directors come in and the first thing they wanna do is say 'look, I have this great idea, I got some torches, I got a cave, I got some smoke, you're gonna love it, I got the chicks in leather, they all got dog collars on, you're gonna love it!!'. Well...that might fit for some things, I'm not denouncing it doesn't work for certain kind of groups and certain music, but it had no place in the song 'Oh, Sherrie'".* He added: *" There's a mystique to music in a radio or a record form that lets each person to see in their mind's eye what it means to them."*

Ultimately, the video for "Oh Sherrie" was so successful it debuted directly at the number one position in MTV's Top 20 Video Countdown in 1984.

Steve was finally content. He had done everything his heart dictated and he was happy that the listeners were enjoying his music just as much as he did." *I'm always trying to expand my music and this solo project serves that purpose for me"*, he said," *Songs can often be like wine, the longer they sit the more charming they become"*.

Walking On High Wire

"Once you love somebody
There's no turning back
It can burn forever, it can haunt you,
Haunt you in the night..."

Steve took some time off after the release of "Street Talk" but not for long - he was already thinking about his next step, as always. He started working on another solo album as he was in a very creative state of mind. The songs were coming along easily and there was no reason to waste any time – Steve got into the studio again and recorded the songs which were going to be on the new album called "Against The Wall". But right after he finished the recordings, the relationship between him and the record label got knotty and eventually the project was set aside. Besides the professional problems, Steve's personal life was also going through some unexpected changes that wouldn't let him focus on his career as much as he wanted to. In June of 1984, a sad break-up with his long time girlfriend, Sherrie, got Steve in the situation of reflecting on the past and threw him in a very delicate emotional state. Some time after their separation, Steve opened up his heart to the fans and made an honest confession through the Journey Fan Club at the time: *"She and I were kind of in and out, but by the time 1985 hit, it was history. We were good for each other, but not right for each other and then, again, not good for each other but right for each other. It happens every day, but it really had never happened to me."*

As if this wasn't enough anguish, tragic news hit his family: his mother, Mary, was diagnosed with a rare neurological disease and the doctors were not too optimistic about her chances to live. Steve was torn apart and the hurt and agony were almost unbearable. He tried to spend as much time as possible with his mother; they were having long talks about everything it was going on in their lives at the time. Although Mary was terminally ill, she tried to put some confidence back in her son's life. She still was Steve's guardian angel just like she's always been and she believed with all her heart that Steve belonged in Journey. Mary knew the band was the perfect place for her son and getting back to work with Journey would've made him feel better. In one of their conversations about Steve's doubts regarding his career, Mary gave her son an answer that made all the difference for his future. It was a highly emotional moment as he recalled it in a later interview: *"When the Street Talk record was done and it had sold a million copies, I said,' Mom, you know, should I go back to do Journey or* *should I do another solo album?' And it wasn't that I was wimping out on my ability to make a decision. I just was confused. So I said 'If I did Journey I wouldn't be able to see you as much, because I'd be in San Francisco writing and recording, If I do a solo project ,I'd be able to record a little bit, come spend a month with you, then record a little bit and do it at my leisure`. And she couldn't speak at that point very well, she could only whisper. And she said the word... "Journey"."*

Steve promised her he would go back to Journey.

Meanwhile, the rumors about the band collapsing were more persistent than ever so Steve felt the need to clear up things. His statement at the time was very honest: *"Journey is and will always remain the mothership! Separate projects aside, we are all members of Journey and that's the way we want it to stay."*

*

March 15, 1984. In San Francisco, in an office at Nightmare Inc. – the company that was managing Journey - six men sat down to talk about the future of their band: Steve Perry, Neal Schon, Jonathan Cain, Ross Valory, Steve Smith and manager Herbie Herbert. There were questions, answers and decisions regarding Journey's next projects. They discussed about writing an album and tour the world every other year and they agreed that each member of the band will have the freedom to work on solo projects. Everything seemed perfectly fine and they all agreed.

By mid '84, Steve started working again with Journey. All of them were energetic and anxious to get that creative ball rolling again. Steve was keyed up: *"To be perfectly honest, I think the band is ready to get excited about itself again. It needed something to rejuvenate itself, and I believe the hiatus was what we all needed."* Steve's belief was that the next Journey album will be better than ever because all five of them learned so many things while working as solo artists. The news of Journey getting together again killed all the previous breaking-up rumors that have been circulating and millions of fans were excited and happy that their favorite band of all time was going to bring back the magic.

Meanwhile, besides the management and the extended staff, there was another institution that was working for the band: Journey's official fan club which was known by the name of Journey Force. This fan-club was started by Tim McQuaid as a hobby, but only in a few years it became the legitimate nerve center of the band.

The Journey Force already had a full-time working staff and it also became the official Journey merchandise store. Based in San Francisco, the hometown of the band, the Force was smoothly organized by its owner and by three other dedicated staff members: Lora Beard, Cindy Poon and Corby Cox. These hard working people were keeping a tight connection between the Journey members and the fans all over the world. It was the official source for all the latest news related to everything the band was doing on and off stage. The Journey Force was getting something like six hundred letters from the fans on a daily basis; people were also able to buy any kind of Journey merchandise - from t-shirts to signed guitars, from tour jackets to concert tickets or autographed posters and albums. It was a all-embracing relationship between the public and the band, a thing both sides needed. The monthly Force Newsletters, which were released to all the Journey Force members, were keeping a clear view on the bands activities and were preventing rumors to get sky-high. Journey was their only client at the time, but later on Journey Force evolved into what is called today the Fan Asylum – a professional company that takes care of some the most important names is today's music business. But back then, Journey was the "engine" of this fan club and 1984 was one of the most eventful years for both Steve as a solo artist and Journey as a band.

While getting ready to begin the writing sessions for the new Journey album, Steve and Jon Cain were approached to write a special song that was going to be a part of a movie soundtrack.*" We contributed the song 'Ask the Lonely' to the film 'Two Of A Kind'. That was a new adventure for me and Jonathan. It's like a growth curve; you feel you must move with it. Finally,' Ask The Lonely' wound up working very well for the film."*

Soon after that, they took time to focus on the songs that were going to end up on the new album. This was a challenging creative step for Journey considering that three years had passed since their last release. In the meantime, rock music evolved and the sound of it was changing. Journey wanted to take a new corner and bring a fresh creative nerve into the songs. Steve had a lot of ideas and he had a certain kind of musical insight that was suppose to reflect a musicianship that reached its peak. A few tunes were sketched and they began rehearsals in the same golden line-up they had during the "Frontiers" era.

In November of 1984, Steve and the band went to Sausalito and rented Plant Studios for the recording sessions of the new album which was going to be named "Raised On Radio". It was a change of concept, considering that every previous Journey album was named with a single word. The idea behind the new name was simple, as Steve told the story: *"Jonathan Cain and I were writing the lyrics for the album and along the way we were looking for a great title for it. We were working on this one song called 'Radio'. One thing led to another and I started telling him how absolutely important radio was in my life. My creative influences, my writing influences, my good times and bad times - all centered around the fact that I had a radio in my car, and I started realizing how important radio was to me. I felt that I'd been 'raised on radio'.... He looked at me and said "Raised On Radio"... and that was it."* This title was also a tribute to all those wonderful radio years when music was getting to the people unaffected by the image. More than that, the band decided not to make any abstract videos for the songs from the new album. Steve was faithful to his standpoint: *"Radio taught me about writing songs, taught Jon to write songs and Neal to play guitar. We were raised on radio."*

Most of the material was already sketched when they went into the studio because Steve, Neal and Jonathan had been writing together at Jonathan's house; some of the songs were really innovative and they had a new edge to them, especially since the band decided to use a drum machine for a more new-fangled sound. The entire recording session was pretty intense. There were songs that were never finished or songs that never made it on the album as Steve was an uncompromising musician - he wanted to keep only the finest tracks. He took over the production chores and was determined to get the very best out of this album. There was pressure along the way, mostly because Steve was searching for the perfect sound that he had in his mind. "Happy To Give" was a tune that obsessed Steve so much he had to record it three times until he was satisfied with the result. Finally, he was able to get across all the feelings he was going through at the time and this song not only became his favorite but it is also one of the top vocal performances of Steve.

While the band was working in the studio, the Journey Force fan club got a very special letter. It was written by a desperate mother whose sixteen year old son was terminally ill with cystic fibrosis. This boy's biggest dream and last wish was to be able to meet his favorite band: Journey.

The fan club called up the guys at the studio and told them about the letter and the boy's situation. Immediately, Steve and the band interrupted their work and decided to fly to Cleveland at the Rainbow Babies and Children's Hospital where Kenny Sykaluc was slowly dying. But before leaving, Journey took something with them – they thought about offering this boy a special gift: a Journey song that was never heard by the public before. "Only The Young" was a track that was originally written for the "Frontiers" album but it was taken out the last minute. Kenny was going to be the first Journey fan to hear this song. The boy was completely transported when he saw the band members in flesh beside his bed. It was like dreaming with his eyes wide open; the band brought him a platinum "Escape" record and a '49ers helmet, then Steve gave Kenny a walkman and played "Only The Young" for him. *"That was really rough"*, remembered Steve, *"because he was in Heaven...you know...he really was in Heaven."* By the time the song was over, the band members were totally touched by Kenny's happiness but they were doing efforts to hold back their tears. Steve was deeply affected by the boy's reaction to the song. He confessed at the time:*" As soon as I stepped out of that hospital room I lost it. Nurses had to take me to a room by myself."*

The very next morning, Kenny Sykaluc died holding his walkman with the new Journey song still playing.

This painful experience left marks is Steve's heart and made him meditate on things he didn't thought about before: *"You can have success in anything you do but you always see to be missing something. Kenny filled in those missing pieces; he was one brave guy."* Journey decided to release "Only The Young" as a single and later, they made it the opening song of the 1986 tour concerts.

After this heartrending episode, Steve went back in the studio with the band – they had to work hard on the new album. But things were not going the right way. Steve was feeling that Journey wasn't capturing the sound they were really looking for. Frequent arguments and tensioned situations led to a hard decision: two of the band members had to quit the project. Ross Valory and Steve Smith left the group and Journey moved on as a trio. After their departure, an audition was set up in order to find some good musicians to fill in; after pondering on what they were looking for, the band hired a new drummer, Larry Londin, the same musician that worked with him on the "Street Talk" solo album; Bob Glaub was hired as the new bass player and Dan Hull for the saxophone additions. In this new studio formula, Journey started recording again.

But by this time Steve's personal life was is trouble as he was more and more concerned about his mother's affliction – she was close to her last days. He couldn't focus on the recordings any longer and at one point he even felt like he should completely stop working on the album and spend his time with his mother. But Mary didn't agree with this interruption and convinced her son to continue the recording sessions. Steve made a promise to his mother and he had to keep it no matter how hard it was to concentrate. He started visiting Mary very often as he knew her days were numbered. *"It was a slow thing and it was painful because I'd watch her life kind of being slowly robbed from her."* Steve went through this ordeal without having a choice. He was working on the new Journey album five days a week, then he would fly down to the Fresno area and spend the weekends with his dying mother. The pressure and the pain were unbelievable: *"Part of it was stressful, making the album, and then part of it was just horrible, watching her get worse."*

On the 4th of December 1985, Mary passed away in the arms of her son. Steve bears in mind that sorrowful moment: *"I told her that if she wanted to go it was ok, because she's been shackled by her body for years. I just kept saying that to her, stroking her forehead...and she passed.".*

Steve biggest supporter was gone that day.

Completely shattered, he returned to Journey and finished the album. It was like he had to abandon himself in hard work in order to survive the agonizing grief he was feeling. The production of the new album got in the final phase and the band along with the management were already doing plans for an extended tour that would bring the new music to the people worldwide. "Raised On Radio" was expected to be released in May of 1986.

1985 was coming to an end and one day, between Christmas and New Year's, Steve went home and found an unexpected message on his phone answering machine. It was from Ken Kagen, a well known manager who always had these major fund-raising ideas. He was asking Steve to take one of the lead parts in this humanitarian project called "USA For Africa". Basically, it was about getting together a group of famous artists to record a song that would be used to raise funds for African famine relief. Steve was touched by the proposition and called Kagen back saying: *"Sign me up".* The final line-up for this project was spectacular. The biggest names of the era were involved such as Tina Turner, Bruce Springsteen, Lionel Richie, Bob Dylan, Michael Jackson, Cindy Lauper, Diana Ross, Bob Geldof and many other platinum record champions. It was a huge undertaking produced by none other than Quincy Jones. Steve was sincerely moved by the fact that he was among the forty-five American superstars chosen to lend their voices to this project. At the beginning of 1986, Steve went to Los Angeles where the song was going to be recorded.

On the night of January the 28th, he entered the A&M Recording Studios and after noticing in amusement the sign outside Studio A which said '*Please check your egos at the door*', Steve rushed into the control room and saw Michael Jackson standing there; he clearly recalled that - it was the moment when he realized how big the event was. Steve looked around in awe and he said: *"Am I dreaming? Am I on drugs or what?"*

When the artists arrived in the studio, there was a piece of tape on the floor for each person to stand on, arranged around six microphones in a semi-circle. The recording session began at 10:30 p.m. on that day and Steve was placed next to his good friend, Kenny Loggins and next to Bruce Springsteen. At one point, Loggins was worried about the way he should sing his line and Steve advised him: *"Just be yourself!"* After several takes, they all stopped for a well deserved break then by 1 a.m. the group started working again. It was a marathon recording session that lasted until almost 8 a.m. the next morning. Even though Steve had finished his part, he didn't want to leave the set not even for a minute because he wanted to see how it all ends. This unique experience impressed him so much that the next day, after a long sleep he made a call. Lionel Richie told the story in an interview at the time: *"I get a phone call at 7:30 pm and it was Steve Perry calling from his L.A. hotel room. I ask him what's wrong and he says that he slept well, he got up and he ordered room service. They brought him breakfast. He sat down. He pulled the silver cover of the food. And then he started crying."*

On March 7th 1985, eight hundred thousand copies of the "We Are The World" single arrived in stores and there were sold out by the first weekend. This wasn't the only reason of joy for Steve - the producers of this project have chosen one of his songs to be on the B-side of the single: "If Only For A Moment Girl".

The record entered the Billboard Hot 100 chart on March 23rd, at number twenty-one. It was the highest debuting single at the time since John Lennon's "Imagine", and reached the number one position in three weeks.

*

In the next months Steve worked frantically with Journey on the final production of the "Raised On Radio" album. Not only the musical concepts changed, but also the appearance of the LP. Steve wanted something suggestive on the cover of the album, something special that would perfectly wrap up the idea of being "raised on radio". The picture was in his memories: *"The radio station in Hanford California... That's where my dad used to sing on live radio shows in the early days. I used to see that station every day on the way to College of the Sequoias when I'd drive to school, and the memory kept on burning in my brain. So when we came up with the title "Raised On Radio," it's the first thing that came into my mind."*

Eleven songs were taken to New York to be mixed and to get their final glow. Steve was confident about the value of each track. He confirmed: *"Journey's style is exactly what you've been hearing all these years. It is capable of change but I don't think it can fabricate a new style, meaning that the band still has to be itself."*

"Raised On Radio" was one of the most awaited Journey albums. After three years of absence, everyone was interested to hear what kind of songs they had been writing. Released in May, the album immediately gave four top hits. The biggest one was "Be Good To Yourself" – *"a Perry-ism"*, as Jon Cain said. However, the song wasn't an easy one to write. They worked on the music and the lyrics for five months. At one point they thought they would never get through with it but one day it just happened. Jon and Steve were in the mixing studio in New York with sound engineer Bob Clearmountain. Cain took a break and while he was showering the melody suddenly became clear in his head. He rushed out the shower and got into the studio with his hair still wet and he played the song to Steve. In less than an hour Steve nailed the song and recorded the most intense vocals ever to be heard. "Be Good To Yourself" became the leadoff single and it was out one month before the album. In a few days it was already in the US Top Ten.

Like always, people were fascinated by Journey's music and they were trying to find out the secret of their success. It seemed that everything they were touching was turning into gold. Steve said in an interview back then: *"There is a definite art form to writing great songs. That is what really matters to me. To write a great song is the most difficult thing of all. And a great song sells itself. You can only damage it by putting it in the wrong singer's hands, or in the wrong band's hands."*

With the official release of the "Raised On Radio" album, Steve had to respond to many questions regarding the new music, the changes, the new line-up, the tour plans; people wanted to know every single detail, reporters were checking the truth of some of the rumors that were flying around, and the experts wanted to know the secret of Journey's success. It was overwhelming but Steve was patient and very honest with every answer he gave.

For the up-coming tour the band got many offers to be sponsored; in the music business that was a money-spinning situation, but Steve's opinion was entirely different. He didn't feel comfortable with selling their name and didn't want to do what every other band was doing. He was valuing music in a spiritual way and didn't want to have a too commercial appearance. *"It just didn't feel correct"*, he said, *"They put their name on the ticket, and put their name on the t-shirt, and you stand in front of the TV and chug-a-lug a soda pop for a commercial. I'm a singer! I'll go down being a singer...and if it takes me having to sell out to be successful, that only tells me that my singing's not working any more, and then I won't do it anymore. That's the way I feel"*, then he added laughing: *"I'll go back to Visalia and teach school!"*

Steve was also asked why he had particularly thanked to the Everly Brothers on the new album. He admitted that the liner note had a special story behind it: *"The reason I personally thanked them on the album was because my mother was very ill at that point when we were doing the album, and we flew her to the Everly Brothers` concert in Lake Tahoe and they dedicated a song to her it was called "Dream"...and it's one of my favorites, and she started crying, so I just wanted to thank them."*

Millions of fans were now excitedly waiting for the big tour to begin after a patiently waiting for three years since they've seen Journey on stage. But before getting on the road, Steve, Neal and Jon had to look for two musicians who would become part of the touring band: a new bass player and a new drummer. For the drummer position, they planned an audition in New York where they met a long list of drummers who wanted a chance to play with the legendary group. After a few days they decided for Michael Baird. Later on, the bass player was chosen as well – Randy Jackson, a musician who's been well known for his work with artists like Whitney Houston, Aretha Franklin and Lionel Richie among many others. Interesting enough, Jackson was not meeting with Journey for the first time – actually he collaborated with Journey as a studio musician and played bass on the "Frontiers" album back in 1983 on the "After The Fall" track. Now he was back as a full time Journey tour bass player. Finally, three weeks before the Raised On Radio World Tour was scheduled to begin, they all went into an unmarked warehouse somewhere in California and heavily rehearsed for the upcoming ride.

*

It was August 23rd 1986, in Calaveras County Fairgrounds, California.

Steve Perry looked around him – he was contemplating the very same place where he received his very first prize in a rock music contest. He and his band at the time won that day in a competition against eighty other bands and his mom Mary was there with him enjoying his success.

Memories came rushing back into Steve's mind as he stood in the same spot he was twenty years ago. A cameraman zoomed on his face and Steve's eyes reflect the nostalgia of those moments as he started speaking: *"It was the summer before I started high-school. I was in a band called The Sullies...and my Mom was managing us at the time. And she got us a chance to come to the Calaveras County Fair and compete in The Battle of the Bands. The prize was Bill Graham would get us a gig at the Fillmore. See this trophy?... I won it."* Steve held up the musical note shaped award, looked into the camera and then he pointed from his left, where he sang two decades ago, all the way to his right where the Raised On Radio stage was set up for that night's concert: *"From there...to over there."*

The Raised On Radio documentary that was filmed on that day of August 23rd was witnessing Journey's first tour day and the first concert which was held at the Mountain Aire Festival at Angel's Camp, California. More so, the film was presenting a close look on Journey's revival after a few years of absence from the music scene. The producers wanted to record the new songs that were going to be played live that night. However, Steve and the band decided before not to make any videos for the new songs and there was enough tension because of the cameras and the recording trucks for the documentary. Lastly, the record company and the manager negotiated with the producers of the documentary and agreed on shooting a segment of that first show at the Mountain Aire. "Girl Can't Help It" and "Be Good To Yourself" were filmed and put out as videos, then later on the tour "I'll Be Allright Without You" was captured on film during a show in Atlanta.

The Raised On Radio Tour was drawing people to the concerts like moths to the flame. The audience was sent to heaven every single night by the phenomenal show put together by the band. But it was more that the music, it was an entire tour concept, starting with the way the stage was looking and ending with the stellar sound of the band. A very attentive witness described at the time what the audience was seeing: *"The stage setting was sparse but stunning - state-of-the-art - visible as much from the back as the front. No amplifiers were in sight. You didn't see the hidden trapdoors, only the silver-colored railings and the walkway behind drummer Michael Baird. Strobe lights flashed as the quintet entered, singer Perry looking like a ring master in his red cutaway over his light blue jeans."*

Steve was having a blast on stage and the people were getting completely loose. He remembered amused the hot summer shows: *"We'd play at some venues where...my God...women's tops would come off and they were like shaking...well, I think they were projecting their own little intimate moment during the songs – yes that has happened especially in the hot summer days in the outdoors on stadiums. It was unbelievable! There were times when I'd even bring a hose on stage and cooled everybody out 'cause everyone was like packed in there and just dying from the heat."*

Steve was mastering the show with incredible power, keeping up the high-energy for almost two hours every night. He was paying attention to every aspect of the concert, starting with the stage and ending with his own presentation. The Raised On Radio Tour Book summed up perfectly Steve's captivating performance: *"Possessing probably the most identifiable voice in contemporary music today, Steve's vocal range goes virtually unchallenged among his peers. One minute he's rocking with the intensity of a 7.3 earthquake, and the next, he's effortlessly seducing an audience with a passionate ballad."* For this tour, Steve also went for a change of looks and this was the moment when the tuxedo became his established mark. The leopard printed shirts from the previous years were gone and now they were replaced with silk shirts with tails and tuxedos that were custom made in San Francisco. He'd been wearing tuxedos in the past too, but this time the tailed coats were almost like a symbol for the entire tour. Especially the red tux would be Steve most identifiable personality mark of the 80s rock music. He recently shared the story of his tailed coats as he was asked about the idea behind the outfit:*" I was watching an old black and white film and saw Fred Astaire wearing black tails. I thought they'd look so cool with jeans and a t-shirt. I had some custom ones made that you can't buy. My tux tails were much longer and the colors of the lining were bright and fun. Something happened to me when I was wearing them."*

On the Raised On Radio Tour, Steve was completely captivating the eyes and the ears of everyone and it seemed that after three years of absence he was even more attached to the fans. But, as usual, this triumph wasn't tolerated by some reviewers who would make a mission out of bashing Journey and its members. Except this time Steve was prepared with the confidence of the artist who knows exactly what he is capable of offering. In one of his statements at the time, Steve confessed that he didn't change his habits and still wasn't looking over the reviews, although Jon and Neal were waking up in the morning and reading everything about the previous night show. Steve explained: *"I can't figure out why they would let someone and I mean some ONE person, have anything to do with their performance. During the show you're getting your review and they tell you, immediately, hot-off-the-press what they think about you! I need no other review."*

Journey was setting up a high-class performance and Steve was completely wrapped up in what he was doing. *"It's like being a pilot"* he said,*" Once you got that fever, you're in trouble. You got to fly, you've got to keep flying. If you don't, you get real antsy."* He was touring the hard way, rarely allowing himself a chance to relax; he was constantly on the run, singing his heart out on stage every night, trying to reach what he wanted.*" I really want perfection. And reaching for it along the way I do believe it makes me reach better heights in myself than I think I would if I didn't strive for that perfection. Unfortunately, I'm never that happy because I never reach perfection but along the way I know I've accomplished something 'cause I'm reaching so far."*

Throughout the tour Steve tried to create a friendly mood between everyone involved because he needed to feel like he was in a family. He recalls funny stories behind the scenes that few people would even guess they were really happening, like the way Steve would be the cook for the entire band and crew after the concerts! *"I used to make pasta for the guys after the show. During the encore, on 'Lovin` Touchin` Squeezin`', one of the crew members was instructed to go ahead and start boiling the water. It was timed perfectly so that after the encore was over and we walked offstage, the water would be boiling. Then I would start frying the garlic and the olive oil with a little bit of onions. When that smell of olive oil and garlic cooking would come down the hall, everyone would get awfully friendly all of a sudden! It would be "Hey, brother, what's happening? How are you doin`?' sniff, sniff, sniff, and I'd go 'Okay. Come on" and I'd make some more and we'd have the whole pasta thing backstage!"* He recalls hilarious stories from the road like the one in Tennessee at this hotel where he witnessed an incredibly amusing episode: *"Ducks went through the lobby everyday. They had ducks that would live in the pond in the center of the lobby and they would bring them in the morning from this special roof top area, they would go down the elevator and it was a big deal! They would roll out a red carpet and they would waddle to the pond and they would stay there the entire day, and then at five o'clock there was a big poo poo hour with the bar and the cocktails and they would roll the carpet up and the ducks would go back up on the roof for the night!"*

But among the amusing memories, there was an unpleasant one that happened during a show in Greensboro which Steve never forgot. Journey was playing "Wheel in the Sky" when suddenly, right in the middle of the song, Steve stopped singing. He put his hand on his face covering his eyes and he seemed to be in some sort of pain. People remember that it took a few moments until the rest of the band realized that something was wrong and stopped playing. Later on, the whole story came out: a drunk man from the audience threw an object towards the stage and hit Steve straight in the eye! It was inconceivable how someone could have done something like that! After a few moments of shock, while the whole venue went silent, Steve took the microphone and asked who hit him with that object which seemed to be a wrist watch. Some people in the audience pointed at the man who was immediately removed by security guards. But Steve was hurt so Journey had a half hour intermission. Eventually, the band came back on stage with Steve feeling ok and they got on with the show.

This tour happened to have some very emotional moments as well, just like the one in Cleveland, at a concert that would remain in Steve's memory for a long time. That night Journey decided to open the show with "Only The Young", a song that had a very special ring to those in Cleveland. They didn't forget the touching story of Kenny Sykaluc, the little boy who was suffering with cystic fibrosis and had his greatest wish fulfilled by Journey right before he died back in 1984, when Steve and the band personally gave Kenny the very first copy of "Only The Young". For that Cleveland concert, the Make A Wish Foundation brought fifty cystic fibrosis patients to enjoy the music of their favorite band. It was a memorable night filled with touching memories.

All in all, the Raised On Radio Tour was going smoothly, but good times didn't last for too long. After five months of non-stop touring, Steve began to feel heavy pressure; Jonathan Cain would admit later: *"People made threats at him, and other things were happening that were very painful. Physically being a singer is very demanding and Steve wasn't just prancing around. He'd bleed a little every time he sang. I think he was tired of bleeding..."*

By the time the Raised On Radio Tour hit December 1986, Steve was completely exhausted and he became conscious that his personal wounds were still there, still hurting. He just couldn't find a way to heal at this rate. He recalls how tough it was to get on stage on the 4th of December 1986, the same day his mother died one year back. The memories were still fresh, the pain was there and he couldn't help it. The honest confession he made back then showed he was a in a very delicate emotional state. He was doing the best he could to be fun and jovial, trying to have a good time, as usual, but it was harder than he thought: *"I didn't want to let this subliminal emotion come through - the reality that this was the eve of the death of my mother. Internally, I knew. I got out there and things were okay. I was having a good time because the people were very energetic and nice, but I still was down at times, thinking that everything was being questioned in my life."* Even so, on that night of December, somebody in the audience made all the difference and changed Steve's state of mind. He told the story of that special someone: *"I was onstage and I was losing it, I was starting to lose face, and worry because I'm just a normal human being and I have emotions, too. And then I saw this little girl, she must have been around 10, who was up front with her mother. She had these thick, little "coke-bottle" glasses, and there she was with this big smile on her face, and she was waving her arms back and forth, though she could barely move because she was crushed among the other people. She was the cutest thing I ever saw, and she was smiling at me, and I looked at her and thought, "You're the queen of the entire evening." I kept looking at her and she got me through the night".*

The tour was following its schedule every night, but instead of going away, the suffering and the weariness were building up inside of Steve. The effort of staying on track was getting bigger with each day of the tour. Looking back at that moment in his life, he described the sensation: *"I felt like I re-entered the Earth's atmosphere without heat tiles on my face. I was burning on my way in. I realized how much fame has sustained me...But I couldn't make that the only thing that makes me feel ok."* Then he added:*" I am no different than anyone else, and life takes no prisoners. Someone wrote that "life is something that happens to you while you're busy making plans." I believe that. (...)"*

He knew he had to stop. He needed to remove his chains.

It was February 1st, 1987.

A Price To Pay

"Lost in twilight, the memories
Precious moments, you and me
We've been old friends, all through the years
Picture postcards, sharing tears..."

On that cold night of February, Journey's history was going to turn an unexpected corner which would throw everybody in a state of confusion. It happened then and there, in Anchorage, Alaska. The last Journey concert at the Sullivan Arena, a rather small place compared to the huge venues they've been playing in through out the Raised On Radio Tour. But the band felt comfortable and they didn't even want to set up their usual tour stage, so they used the standard stage setting from the Sullivan Arena.

No one knew this was the last concert, except for the band and a few staff members of the Journey Force Fan Club. It was going to be the last time when people would see the band members touring together.

Steve got ready to step into the spotlight just as he did every night. Nothing gave away his extreme exhaustion and he didn't let anyone see how depressed he really was. It was their show and Steve wanted to keep his promise he once made to the fans that they will never be disappointed by a Journey concert. It just had to be perfect and everyone out there had to leave the venue in high spirits.

Being aware that this was going to be the last Journey show, Lora Beard from Journey Force flew in from San Francisco and was in the audience that night. She remembered and shared some special moments: *"It was kinda nostalgic... The band played a bunch of tunes they don't usually play like Stand By Me, Kansas City, and it was a wild show.(...) Steve decided to run down the stairs and out into the crowd. I thought Journey's head of security was going to have a heart attack. Everything ended up well, but it was quite exciting for awhile. I think it was also at this show that the band pulled one on Steve when he was doing the intro to "Oh Sherrie." Remember how he would come out wearing his "Oh Sherrie" hat as he began that song? Well, he came out with the hat, but didn't realize that behind him the rest of the band members were also wearing the same hat. The crowd was laughing and he couldn't figure out why and he turns around and sees the guys wearing those hats. He was doubled over laughing.* " Then, when finally the show was coming to an end, underneath the stellar performance there was a lot of anxiety. They all felt the need to have a few giggles in order to release the pressure. During "Faithfully", which was the second encore, the entire road crew came out on stage and sang the final lines with Steve and the band. Lora Beard recalls another amusing moment: *" Two of the guys on the crew ran up and gave Steve a double wet-willy as he was trying to sing. He was laughing so hard he could hardly sing."*

But the fun didn't last too long. The lights went down, the people left and it was quiet. Jonathan Cain bared in mind the image of the lobby at the Anchorage Sheraton where he stood for a long time signing autographs until the last fan was gone. Cain stated later: *"I knew it was over…It was a sad, sad night".* Steve Perry said his goodbyes to all and then he left.

After ten years of professional singing, the Voice was silent.

*

"Steve Perry had to stop...to find out what was left standing after a very large circus ride. I couldn't really explain why I had to jump off the merry-go-round and it's still difficult to explain why... But I think one of the reasons I had to do it...I had to do it for my life. I had to stop, I had to find out if I loved singing, because I worked so hard for so long."

This is what Steve said in his first filmed interview after seven years of staying away from the music business. Since that night in 1987, he spent his time struggling to get his life back together, trying to heal his wounded heart and re-evaluating himself on a deep level. For so many years he had shared his voice and his life with the world, he stood on the peak and wanted to reach even higher without noticing that real life was getting away from him. That was the reason why for almost seven years he shut the door on everything he had done and pondered on his existence. It was important for him to find out the truth about his life as it reached a point of no return. But this was his personal battle which no one knew. After that last concert in Alaska, there was nothing left to say for him. Looking back, he confessed that he suffered a massive job burnout and he couldn't find the power to go on any longer. Steve had a talk with Neal and Jon after the Raised On Radio Tour was over and he told them he needs to quit. *"They wanted to keep going and I just couldn't; I didn't feel good about it, but what could I do?"*

After the 1987 tour stopped, the world went crazy. The news of Journey breaking up got to the fans right away and rumors started spreading like wildfires through all the channels. Steve recalls the psychosis: *"They said I had throat cancer. People on the street would walk up and say to me they were sorry"*. But there was an explanation for the reason why that rumor started: *"What happened was, when I was taking my mother around different hospitals to radiology, people would see Steve Perry sitting there. They didn't know what Steve Perry's mother looked like, but they would see me sitting there and put two and two together and they started figuring throat cancer"*. Sadly, all that nonsense affected his family along with him; people didn't realize that the rumors they were spreading was the fastest way to harm his personal life: *"One time I'll never forget, my grandfather called me crying on the phone because he had gotten a phone call form a friend of his who had seen me at a medical center. The rumor was that I had throat cancer and that I was in the x-ray ward. Grandpa was crying and saying 'Why didn't you tell me?' and I said 'Grandpa, I don't know what you're talking about.' I explained to him that I was there with Mom and even then he didn't believe me."*

Questions, suppositions, rumors – everything was centered on Steve's departure from Journey. People were constantly making up all kinds of scenarios but the truth was uncomplicated: Steve was simply… human. He had a broken heart, he had mixed-up feelings and he certainly had a limit of endurance. Behind the famous rock star there was a sensitive man who had to abruptly face the realities of his own life. He confessed in all sincerity: *"There were so many things happening to me at the time. During the last years of Journey my mother had gotten progressively worse and she passed away while I was doing the vocal for the Raised On Radio album. On top of that I had lost a relationship that didn't work out. So we went out on tour to promote Raised On Radio and it was only then that I realized what happened. I have never dealt with any of the personal stuff before. It's so easy to keep busy and not feel what's going on, especially if you're in the music business."*

After quitting the stage in 1987, Steve Perry didn't sing at all for two years. He isolated himself and thought about giving up music for good. It was hard for him to figure out what was left after that wild ride he took for ten long years, so he felt that the best way to get his feet on the ground was to simply live the life he was given. At the time, his most relaxing hobby was riding the motorcycle a lot – it was a way of getting his mind off of things. *"I went back to my hometown and I got my motorcycle out of storage and I cruised around the central San Joaquin Valley, which is nothing but country roads, small towns that I grew up in. And I just had to reflect on what had happened".* Besides that, Steve got to spend some quiet times in the safety of his home recovering from the tremendous weariness he's been accumulating over the years. After a while he tried to put some excitement back in his personal life by learning how to fly helicopters. He would get assistance from a pilot and he'd fly over Yosemite enjoying the incredible view or cruising along the beautiful California coastline. During that period of time he felt the need to go back a few times to Hanford, his hometown, and even got to spend there a whole week hanging out at the local fair, meeting old friends and having some fun.

At one point Steve decided to visit his grandparents' country, Portugal. Reconnecting with his family's homeland gave him a sensation of security he didn't felt in a long time. After all those hectic years, Steve was becoming aware of the simple pleasures of life. All that painful agony that grew inside of him over the years was slowly disappearing and the ease he was feeling made him comfortable; one time he even fell asleep on this lovely deserted beach somewhere in the Azores Islands. However, it wasn't all sunshine and blue skies…As 1989 was coming to an end, Steve got sad news about one of the most beloved member of his family. His 88 year old grandfather, Manuel, was irreversibly sick. Vavou, as Steve used to call him, was one of the few close relatives that he had left and he was especially connected to his grandfather to whom he owed so much of his early education and support. Manuel Quaresma had been like a father to Steve through the years so now he felt it was time to return all the love he had received from him. Steve moved down to Southern California and took care of his grandfather until his last day. It was almost like a silent apology for all the time he couldn't be there for his loved ones.

That was life, a normal way of living with the goods and the bads that came along and Steve was simply trying to deal with everything day by day.

After a while, he knew he just needed to get out more and enjoy life, meeting friends and going to some concerts or, in his own words, *"putting some experience back in my life"*. Steve was having a good time watching others sing as an alternative to all those years when he was the entertainer. The sensation was great and he really took pleasure in staying in the audience for a change. But he was such a well-known face that it was almost impossible to get away unnoticed and it wasn't only the fans who recognized him, but the musicians as well. That`s how one night, to his surprise, he was invited to join the Everly Brothers live on stage! The band was having a concert at Great America and Larry Londin was on tour with them at the time. Larry was a very good friend of Steve`s as they have been working together on the last Journey album and on Steve`s solo project back in 1984. So that night Steve was asked to join the Everly Brothers up on stage and he has a vivid memory of that moment: *"I was really shocked because I've been told they have never asked anyone to come onstage. They asked me to come on and sing 'Let It Be Me'. It sounded like the Everly Brothers, the Sons of The Pioneers, and Journey combined. It sounded great and it was really, really a highlight and a lot of fun because I hadn't sung in front of people since the tour ended."*

But that wasn't the only time when Steve got to sing on stage with his fellow musicians. Next it happened at the Shoreline Club in Northern California, where Steve had another thrilling surprise. He was in the audience watching a Bon Jovi concert when Jon Bon Jovi saw him and invited him immediately to join the band for a first-class jam! Steve sincerely enjoyed that special night: *"I was really, really pleased that Jon was so insistent on me going out there and doing that"*, Steve recalls, *" I was saying 'Jon, this is your crowd; they love you. This is your show. I just came to watch you guys play.' He kept on going 'no, no, no, no. You've gotta come up, man. We'll do this Sam Cooke tune "Bring It On Home To Me"*. They felt so good on stage together that before knowing it they got to play more songs; one of them was

"Reach Out" by the Four Tops, a song that Steve used to do with Journey on their tours. It was obvious that Steve was absolutely delighted to be able to sing again as he hadn't been up on a stage for sometime. He felt like having a little fun for a change: *"I grabbed the mike and said to myself, 'I'm just going to go out there and enjoy myself.' And I did; I enjoyed it very much"*. Yet, that wasn't going to be the only big surprise of the night – Steve recalls an emotional moment while he was onstage with Bon Jovi: *"A friend of mine who works on the Bon Jovi crew gave me a microphone that he had for years. I used it on the Infinity Tour and I couldn't believe that he had this same mike and I recognized it. It really was a fun thing and it was great to hear and see the crowd's response. It made me very happy!! "*

Little by little, the passion for music was growing again inside Steve's heart so he decided to turn his attention on one of his older projects which he gave up right before starting to record the "Raised On Radio" album with Journey. Back then, before choosing to return to Journey, Steve was determined to do another solo album as a follow up of the success he had with "Street Talk". But the songs he recorded back in 1984 were shelved because he made a promise to carry on his career with Journey. Now that he was on his own again, that solo project was a big temptation. The songs only needed some touch-up paint in order to be ready. He was planning to produce the album along with his old friend Randy Goodrum and the band was going to be the same he'd worked with on the "Street Talk" project. Steve had already twelve songs which were going to make his second solo album named "Against The Wall". But although he put a lot of effort and passion in this new project, the music business wasn't always as considerate as it was supposed to be - things just didn't go the right way between him and the recording label and the album was stopped in its tracks and it wasn't released to its full length. Many years later, Steve decided to officially release a few of those songs. The absolute quality of the tunes made everyone regret that "Against The Wall" didn't came out as a full record. *"The album would have made some noise"*, he said in a later interview.

The beginning of the 90s found Steve looking more confidently into his future because the past made him reassess a lot of his main beliefs. He was honest with himself and the people around him; he would confess back then that he had lost the passion for something that he loved doing. His reluctance also came from the fact that he had lost most of the people who he dearly loved, and that made him reflect on the fragility of life in general. His old principles had changed. He didn't believe anymore in the "immortality" feeling he got when he reached a certain status. *"I learned a few things about immortality upon re-entering the atmosphere. I lost some of my heat tiles on the way in. So now I'm a little singed, but a lot better."*

Steve was still on the mend, still trying to get used to everyday life, taking time to visit family and friends and doing all the things that usual people were doing. But he was soon going to discover that it wasn't an easy thing for him to have a private life because people were recognizing him wherever he would go. For them he was Steve Perry - the rock star, although he still didn't looked at himself that way: *"I just think 'I'm Steve Perry, I'm just me'. But people remind me that, no, I'm **Steve Perry**, and I know that. It's not that I mind being recognized. I enjoy people. There are times when I go away to hide, but I do that in different places."*

Although he was trying to keep away from the past, Steve was sometimes getting in touch with his former band mates. One day he got to talk with Randy Jackson, the bass player who worked with Steve and Journey on the Raised On Radio Tour. While discussing current music, they had a talk about great guitar players and Jackson mentioned Nuno Bettencourt who was playing with Extreme at the time. Steve knew him and thought highly about his guitar skills. The name Bettencourt was of Portuguese heritage and Steve asked Randy if Nuno was really Portuguese. Jackson said that Nuno was coming from a traditional Portuguese family just like Steve was. That was really appealing to Steve, so the next thing he wanted was to get in touch with Nuno. Steve remembers he got his number and when he called Nuno wasn't home as he was touring with Extreme at the time – but Steve recalls having a great conversation with Nuno's mother. Ultimately, Steve reached Nuno and they got along just great. *"He speaks Portuguese and so do I, so next time we started talking and we became friends on the phone. He came to town and we got together, we started a song and the next thing you know we were planning when we could continue that. Finally, I flew to Massachusetts, we went to a little studio and got some musician friends of his and started coming up with some ideas. We recorded a song. It was Nuno, Gary Cherone (Extreme's vocalist) and myself that got together. Then we recorded the song and it's a great tune,"Always" – it was him and I singing with acoustic guitars."* However, Nuno Bettencourt wasn't the only artist with whom Steve worked during this time. One day, Mick Mars, the guitar player of the rock band Motley Crue asked Steve to come and hang out with the band for a rehearsal session. Steve accepted and it turned out to be a fun experience! Steve recounts the story: *"I went down just to sort of hang and we started jamming. I hadn't done that in a while. Those cats play loud! I mean Journey was also loud but these cats really get it in! The room was a little too small and it was filled with sound. Tommy Lee's drums are so incredibly large, they sound so pronounced, it's wonderful! Then there was Nikki`s bass and Mick's guitar was screaming. We jammed on an idea and then we did a cover tune. We did 'Stand By Me'! Yeah, Motley Crue and Steve Perry doing 'Stand By Me'! It was just exploding, it was big! We had a great time."*

Steve was enjoying his new way of life at his own pace and everything seemed perfectly fine. Then one day it just happened. A tragedy was going to bring Steve and Journey together on a stage again.

*

In one of the extensive interviews Steve gave to Lora Beard and Cyndi Poon from the Journey Force at the beginning of the '90s, he went back in time where the memories of his career with Journey were locked. He remembered a story that happened many years back at the Oakland Coliseum at a Day On The Green show where Journey had a concert. He recalled Bill Graham, the famous promoter, who was standing backstage with them. Bill was ready to go on stage and speak to the huge audience. *"To come to San Francisco and play a Bill Graham show and have Bill bring you on stage…it was a classic thing"*, remembers Steve, *" So I looked at him and I said 'Bill, introduce us!' Bill looked at me and said 'What?' and I said 'Come on, introduce us!' Then he holds up two fingers. I'm thinking 'Two fingers? What is this guy doing?' I look over and he holds up two fingers again. And I said 'What?' and he says 'Two dollars. I charge two dollars'. I started laughing but he was dead serious. I had to borrow two bucks because I didn't have any money in my tails. I gave Bill the money and he went out there and he introduced us. Then he came back and said 'I'm gonna keep this, I'm gonna keep this' and I bet he did!"*

But that was happening long ago, at the beginning of the 80s.Now it was 1991 and Bill Graham was gone. Steve was in Los Angeles when he heard about Bill's tragic accident: a helicopter crash that took his life away before time. Graham was one of the most prolific promoters in the United States and his shows, "Bill Graham Presents", were bigger than life. He had a long time professional relationship with Journey and a lot of the greatest shows of the band were set up with Graham's input. His death was a big loss for the rock business and it was decided that he would be honored in a majestic show called "Laughter, Love & Music", which was going to be held in San Francisco's Golden Gate Park at the Polo Fields. Steve immediately knew that this was going to be a very special tribute and he thought it would be great if Journey would get together and sing "Lights" for Bill. Steve didn't hesitate – he picked up the phone and called Neal Schon: *"I discussed with him and he sounded like he was really into it. Then I called Jonathan who was into it as well. So we got together and we did it. It was a very emotional thing to be there."*

The huge show began at 11 a.m. on the 3rd of November 1991 and it gathered on the same stage some of the biggest names that Bill Graham worked with throughout his career: Grateful Dead, Santana, Neil Young, Joan Baez, Jackson Browne and so many more. That was the first time since

1987 when the three members of Journey met on a stage. They played special versions of "Lights" and "Faithfully" in front of one the biggest crowd ever: five hundred thousand people were attending Bill Graham's tribute show. Steve was a bit nervous about getting on stage after all that time but he got over that feeling pretty quickly: *"I guess it's like riding a bicycle"*, he confessed, *" After you do something for so long, it just comes back. I was really delighted to see that a lot of people knew who we were. We were really well received."*

However, as soon as their moment was over they all went their separate ways again. Although rumors started flying around and many Journey fans got their hopes high thinking that maybe the band was ready to get back again, a reunion wasn't going to happen soon. The good old rock and roll days were just sweet memories from another life.

For The Love Of Music

1991 **was a year** that ended up with an unexpected event that Steve never forgot. He was involved in a scary story that occurred in Los Angeles where he was living at the time. On the 30ᵗʰ of December he was driving up Highland in his 1974 white Cadillac which he affectionately called the Love Lounge. Steve was very fond of that car because it was a gift from his grandfather. As he was driving through the city at one point he had to stop at a red light on Sunset Boulevard. Suddenly, the driver next to him yelled *"Hey, you're on fire!"*. Steve was seeing smoke around but he assumed it was from someone else's car. But then he realized that the smoke was coming out from under the hood of his own car! Steve didn't panic too much as he thought it must be a minor leaking problem. He parked the car on the right side of Sunset and wanted to see what's wrong when big flames started to build up the hood! Steve recalls the fright: *"I really thought there was a chance it was going to blow up! I jumped out of the car and ran about a block down the street and I just had to stand there and watch it burn. It was a powerless feeling. So I just sat there and watch it burn."* Through all the confusion and the despair of loosing his car like that, Steve was calmed down by a total stranger:" *I was walking around in circles in front of this building and a short Hispanic lady comes up to me - she couldn't have been taller that my hip- and she says 'Don't worry. God take care of you' I looked at her and said 'Pardon me?' – because she caught me off guard and she said 'Don't worry, you're ok. That's what's important. You can get another car, but you...you're ok'. I looked at her and I said 'You're right!'. That hadn't crossed my mind because I was just thinking about saving my Love Lounge."* Eventually, the whole episode ended without Steve being injured in anyway but, sadly, his white Cadillac was forever gone. It wasn't the greatest way to finish a year but Steve was thankful that it didn't turn out worse.

Without his favorite car but with new energy, Steve started off 1992 thinking more and more about writing songs and singing. He was experiencing desires he thought he had lost forever. The love for music was still there, intact, just waiting for the right moment to wrap him up again. *"I was bored without music in my life"*, he confessed, *"People would stop me on the street and ask, 'Are you Steve Perry? What happened to you?' That helped me to want to come back and make music again."*

Steve was getting entertained about the idea of returning to the music business and he was analyzing options. However, he had a certain idea of a musical environment that always made him click. Steve has always loved working with people in a band situation, so he started thinking about finding the right musicians and put a band together just like he did back in 1984 for the "Street Talk" solo album. The reasons were clear, as he stated back then: *"You can get yourself a great-sounding section, but it's all about spirit. There are a lot of groups that aren't proficient individually, but collectively there's a spirit. I wanted to have a band feeling."* The partnership with other musicians was getting Steve back in a creative environment that was very important to him - all through the year of 1992, Steve wrote some songs with a few musicians like Mark Spiro, Peter Collins, ex Baby-drummer Tony Brock, Alice Cooper's first guitarist Dick Wagner with whom Steve wrote two songs, and of course, Extreme's guitarist Nuno Bettencourt with whom Steve had a very special friendship.

However, Steve was now focused on searching for fresh musicians who would be willing to record and to tour as well. He was aware that it's going to be a pretty hard thing to get, because a lot of the musician out there were having a great time sitting in the studio and doing recordings but they were not motivated enough to get on the road and adapt to the rigors of touring. The first step he made was after he followed the advice of Cindy Poon from the Journey Force staff, who knew Paul Taylor, the former keyboard player of the rock group Winger. Cindy had a good intuition and she felt that Steve and Paul could be a good artistic match. That`s how one day, through a very early morning call, she told Steve that he should look up Paul Taylor and get together with him for some song writing . At the time Taylor had just left Winger and he was available. Steve took his phone number and called him. They met not long after that call and Steve was very pleased to discover a very special musician. It was exactly what he needed. *"Paul is a very creative guy. He comes up with one of the most beautiful chord changes I've heard in a long time. I'll go 'We need something right here, don't think- just play it' and he'll do something great."*

The hardest part was finding a good guitar player. Of course there were a lot of great guitarists out there, they were very talented and technical but Steve was looking for that special sound, that special feeling behind the skillfulness and it was a long time before the right musician came along. It happened that Randy Jackson, the ex- bass player from the 1986 Journey tour, who was now a Sony Music executive, knew that Steve was looking for a guitarist so one day he sent Steve a tape with this young musician by the name of Lincoln Brewster. He had recorded some songs, they were not quite polished but for Steve was enough. *"I was listening to the tape and I could feel that there was something behind his playing. There was soul in there."* Steve called him up right away and after Brewster got over the shock of talking with the famous Steve Perry, they both decided to meet in Los Angeles. And that was the way it all began. Steve, Paul and Lincoln hung out together for a while, jamming and writing down some ideas. They were getting along very well and it already was a wonderful kinship between the three of them. After a while Steve was longing to move further and get the band rolling for real. He started looking for a drummer who would click with them, but at first he couldn't find one to fulfill his expectations. Steve's high sense of rhythm requested a certain kind of a drummer. But just like fate is following its path without digression, one day someone knocked at the door of the studio where Steve and his friends were jamming. He remembers that everything happened very fast: *"This guy, Moyes Lucas, knocks on the door and says he wants to audition.(...) So Moyes came in and set up and we could tell from watching him tune up his kit that he was different. We knew right away. We started jamming and we did write a song then."*

With the new drummer being hired in the band, things were going the right way and Steve was getting more and more excited about working on a new album and do everything that would come along with a project like that. Meanwhile he was looking at two bass players that were equally good: one of them was Mike Porcaro and the other one Larry Kimpel who was a local Los Angeles bass player. A few songs were already getting ready to be recorded so Steve finally decided it was time to officially start working on his second solo album. This was also a very emotional step for him but it felt right. In a 1994 filmed interview he honestly admitted: *"I would say that I feel more and more comfortable with these new songs than I felt in a long time. I really didn't have a lot to say in seven years. I didn't wanna make a record just because it was time to turn up the crank, you know? I had nothing to say. I was dry. I don't feel dry anymore".* The passion for music was there again and Steve's creative side pushed him to pursue his intuition." *The only thing I can do",* he said, *"is follow my heart and literally do the best I can to pour the emotion to each song."*

In less than eight months, Steve and the band finished something like thirteen songs that were mostly written in a rehearsal situation. He was enthusiastic about the way the new band fell together: *"It was very collaborative; there are so many songs that were written in a group rehearsal situation, because that was the best place to test-drive them. Like a fast car."* About the way the new songs were coming along, Steve confessed: *"I hear a song finished the moment we start doing it. When Paul or Lincoln come up with an idea, or Moyes, we're playing together and we start an idea, then I hear the direction pulling on how I should follow it; and it isn't something that I calculate ,it's just there."*

Besides writing the melody lines, Steve was feverishly working on the lyrics. That was one of his ways of reaching out to the people and make honest confessions about some truthful experiences – there were little stories about the things that were going on in his life at that point. *"I think that writing these things down it kind of breaks the door down and lets air into some corners of my soul"*. Steve disclosed the fact that this new album was more emotionally exposed than anything he'd ever done before. Although this was making him a bit more vulnerable, it was the only way to grow. *"I wrote "Missing You" with Tim Miner, which Larry Dalton did the string arrangements for, and conducted, and we did that in Dallas. That was one of the songs that was written in a day"*. This song obviously had some of Steve's early influences, like Marvin Gaye or Sam Cooke – an attempt to get the soul these singers had in their voices.

The rehearsal sessions were also a great source of inspiration - "Donna Please" was a song born that way. Steve remembers one day while rehearsing, Paul Lincoln started playing some beautiful chord changes that inspired him to follow that line: *"I heard the melody and some lyrics, 'You are here, in my voice, inside of me'. And then I got together with Stephen Bishop, - who I've wanted to write with but have never had an opportunity to - and I wrote the lyrics with him."*

Steve was getting ideas from various life situations, just as it happened with the song called "Somewhere There's Hope" which was written with Paul, Moyes and Lincoln; it was a song for those who have lost their way doing things that kept them running in the cold world, a song for the people who are out there on the streets and they're dangerously close to not getting back. Moyes Lucas, Steve's drummer, has a vivid memory about the situation when 'Somewhere There's Hope" was written: *" We wrote that song after hanging out at a Toto rehearsal, after Jeff Porcaro had died. There was a feeling of something passing and something missing...We were full of emotion when we got back to our rehearsal studio, and we just started talking about Jeff and Toto, and we ended up going to the instruments and that song came out."* In one of the songs, called "Young Hearts Forever", Steve added a special part – in fact the end of the song was Steve's tribute to Thin Lizzy, one of his favorite bands, and also an homage for one of his best friends, Phil Lynott. The song faded out with the famous riffs of Thin Lizzy's hit "The Boys Are Back In Town".

Steve didn't hesitate to explain the many reasons why he had to share his feelings on each song. Perhaps the most controversial song of all was "Anyway". Steve has been working on the song with Tim Miner and he felt this was a fitting tune for a certain feeling that he's been keeping inside of him for a long time. Steve knew that sooner or later he had to let it surface but he wasn't quite sure he was ready to write about that. "Anyway" was meant to be a song about his experience with Journey and finally, Steve decided to be honest about the whole situation. He was asked about the meaning of this song and he made a sincere statement: *"I wanted to pay respect and I wanted to talk about my portion of the insanity of the relationship with my ex-compatriots.(...)In a very honest way, without sounding disrespectful or camp it was to give a heartfelt admission of my part of the insanity. We were a band. It's a relationship. You spend all that time together and you're not allowed to fight...?"*

Steve's new band was everything he could've wished for. They were not only gifted musicians but they were getting along great as people. Besides writing and rehearsing, they would spend a lot of time together talking about matters of life, joking and having a good time, enjoying a friendship that would be cherished by each and everyone of them. Lincoln Brewster pleasantly remembers how Steve would take him to a Barbra Streisand concert or to Disneyland just for fun; Steve was a high-spirited person with a huge sense of humor and everyone was feeling comfortable next to him both on and off work schedule. His new band mates soon discovered the perfectionist in Steve: he wouldn't stop until he'd found the exact musical style he was looking for. The creation process was very important and Steve was very excited that he had such a great setting to write in. He remembers the songs were conceived in a small room with just a keyboard they were turned into complete songs: *"They were born big. That's why they sound the way they do. I love working in that situation. You get to hear it, you get to feel it, you get to stand in front of it".*

More than anything Steve wanted to create state-of-the-art music and for that he was asking for a complete artistic workout; that's why he hired a vocal coach for Lincoln in order to improve his background voice input. Lincoln admitted it was a giant step forward for him as a musician. Being able to better control his voice gave him more confidence as a musician and helped him later to express himself with greater power. Moyes Lucas was also enjoying the great experience of working with Steve. He confessed later: *"Steve taught me valuable lessons about dealing with the music business at that level, and how to be secure in what you do and who you are. My first impression of Steve was that he was a dedicated spontaneous sort of guy, and music was his life".*

Steve was now more relaxed. With the right musicians next to him and with the pleasure for singing coming back into his life, he knew he could move on to a next stage as he felt like he was born again from his own ashes: *"I think there's gratitude in my life,* he would confess at the time, *"I'm just grateful for so many things I have...And I'm not talking about cars and houses or anything that equates "strange medicine" .I'm talking about things that matter."*

Steve Perry's new solo album was going to be called "For The Love of Strange Medicine" after one of the songs from the album. This title sounded very thought-provoking to many people and Steve has been asked many times about a possible message hidden in that choice of words. His first inspirational moment was when he saw a work of art: *"There was a painting called "For The Love Of Strange Medicine" done by a gentleman ,I think Tom Rose was his name – it was a collage of a million different things and I just remember looking at it and feeling that if there's ever a place that most of the lyrics on this record come from, it would be that title; what it is to me is the things I have done in my life fore the love of strange medicine. The strange medicine can be anything: too many cars, too many houses, not enough money, the wrong relationship for the wrong reasons, even trying to be famous can be strange medicine...or when you sit in a studio for hours. You do some funny things for the love of strange medicine"*. Steve's answers were honestly reflecting his personal saga: *"More times than I'd care to mention, I have hinged my happiness on outside stuff - strange medicine. Whether it's gambling, or relationships, or a new car or winning the lotto, whatever. It's all strange medicine because it only works so long"*. He concluded: *" I'm not saying I've made it to the top of the Himalayas and I've got my white robe on and I'm cured. I'm still alive and living the same life you are"*.

*

The news of Steve Perry getting back in the spotlight again after seven years of silence caused a tremendous stir especially among the longtime fans. In everyone's mind Steve's name was forever linked with Journey and they were confused at first. Tons of rumors have been circulating since that last Journey concert in Alaska and now they didn't know what to believe anymore. Was Steve Perry coming back to do a solo record or was he getting ready for a reunion with Journey? Didn't he loose his voice after all? Would he start touring again? Without Journey? It was a turmoil which needed to be cleared up before it got out of line. Steve decided to voice his intentions through an official outlet and so, in a short while, S.P.I.N. was born. The Steve Perry Info Network was something like a PR office put together by two of the most loyal friends of Steve, Lora Beard and Cyndy Poon, former members of the Journey Force staff. Through S.P.I.N., Steve was in touch with the people, keeping them properly informed about his plans and his work. Now that S.P.I.N. was up, the questions started flowing and, as expected, everybody wanted to know what happened with Steve throughout the past years, where has he been, what was he working on – the fans were enthusiastic about his comeback and they were eagerly waiting to hear his music and his voice again. Steve was getting hundreds of messages everyday and all that incredible love he was receiving from the people was like a balm to his heart. Having the band he dreamed of and the support of his fans, Steve was in his best creative mood after a long time.

Between interviews and photo sessions, they were working hard to get the album ready. Steve and his band went to record the songs in several studios like the Third Encore Studio in Los Angeles, then in Burbank and Dallas; Jim "Jimbo" Barton, known for his work with Queensryche, was in charge with the production chores as well as Tim Miner and then Steve himself was involved in every single aspect of the creation as he supervised closely the entire project. By the end of 1993, in a very cold and snowy New York, fighting a rebel flu, Steve spent almost two months mixing and mastering his album, working long hours everyday to get the best out of each song. The album had to be ready for its release which was set for March of 1994.The critics as well as the millions of fans were more than eager to listen to Steve's new solo effort and to find out what was his musical approach after all those years of silence. Steve made a few confessions about his personal feelings on the new album, although it was hard to assess his own work: *"It's hard to evaluate my music. I think I am too close to it. Each song* has got something special that I've lived with, through every process from the writing, to the to the arranging, to the recording, to the singing, to the mixing and mastering – I've lived with each song so they're like children, you know...I like them all for different reasons."

The first song taken from the album and released as a single was "You Better Wait". Steve had a weakness for this track and he believed in the message he wanted to pass on to the listeners. This song was one of the first ones that he and his new band had written together at rehearsals. But the song was always changing, meaning that the final form for it was found the last minute during the mixing phase. The beautiful vocal line which opens the song was added right before the final touch-up. *"There's maybe as many as twenty Steves in there. When it gets to the point where it all phases together, you don't need to add any more. I just sounds so creamy".* The song topped the charts right away bringing the new album up for Gold. The record was released on the 19th of July 1994, it was one of that summer's best sellers and it sure got everyone talking about The Voice again. Steve was specific about what his album was all about as he intended to make it entertaining and above all diverse. He had his reasons for that: *"I hate those albums where track one is exactly the same as track 10. A record should be like a meal; it should start off with a little salad, go onto the main course and close with a nice dessert".* Then he added: *"As a singer there are many different things I want to sing, I'm not covered with just one kind of music. I have two different kinds of music in my mind and I want to get involved in so many things vocally. It's been a challenge to sing a ballad and then to sing "You Better Wait."*

After the album was released, people discovered Steve's new vocal manner on the album. It was rather different from his past performances with Journey and the questions about this change started pouring, just like it happened to him a decade before, when he recorded "Frontiers" with Journey and then his first solo album "Street Talk": *"When I was doing the music in Journey that was the vocal character that those particular songs needed. When I'm doing these new songs it's a different character because these songs needed a different enhancement".*

Steve was completely comfortable with the way he put together the new album and now that his project was completed and released to the public he was seriously thinking of living his next year of life on the road, doing what he loved the most: connecting with his audience. He admitted that making records was the necessary evil to get in front of the people, then he added: *"If I could just get out and play live everywhere and not make a record, I probably would. But sometimes...I just like staying in the studio and not leaving...It's a safe place."*

*

October 21st, 1994, Milwaukee, Wisconsin.

The Riverside Theater was jam packed and people were getting anxious as all their attention was focused on the stage. Sass Jordan, the singer who's been in charge with the opening act for that night's show, ended her performance and as the lights went down on stage everybody could feel the tension in the air. The audience was counting the minutes until the big moment. They all have been waiting eight years for this to happen. Then, all of a sudden, a blue light brushed the stage and a deep keyboard sound coming from everywhere filled the air. A woman in the back row whispered "Oh my God" when Steve Perry walked on stage wearing the same charming smile which people loved so much. In a black t-shirt and torn-up jeans, Steve's looks were different from the times he was Journey's front man. Now he had incredibly long hair down to his waist and an exotic charm which suited him so well; he was walking and breathing like a rock star. Everyone could feel the way he commanded the stage and he was doing that in a perfectly natural way; after all those years, Steve was the same powerful entertainer like he'd always been. It looked like all that time he'd spent away from the stage hasn't affected him at all – the audience had the feeling that his last gig was just yesterday.

Steve and his band started out with "Only The Young" and "Girl Can't Help It", two of the most loved songs from the Journey era. All the beautiful memories came back through those songs, both for Steve and his fans. It was magnificent. Steve went to the edge of the stage and looked around with his eyes sparkling with joy. *"I have died and gone to Heaven..."* he said, *"I see real people in front of me! Thank you for inviting us to your city!"* Then Paul Taylor started playing a beautiful melody line while Steve's warm voice filled people's hearts with the emotion of true music...*"I remember your face...I remember your smile...Your sweet embrace..."* Steve started singing one of his most successful songs of his solo career, "Oh, Sherrie", and the audience's response was fabulous – they sang every word along with Steve and the whole atmosphere was electric." Send Her My Love" brought tears in people's eyes and when "Lights" came on, the place went wild – it was a magic night, such a special warmhearted feeling that was obviously going back and forth between Steve and his fans. Those eight years of absence meant nothing because it was like he never really left. Singing along, clapping and swaying to the rhythms, everyone was absorbing Steve magnificent voice and for almost two hours people got lost in the music - by the time the show was over he was walking on a bed of roses, hundreds of beautiful red roses that were thrown on stage by his fans. Steve was overwhelmed by the way he was welcomed.

One of the most fun moments of the shows was the "tuxedo episode": at one point during the concert a red tuxedo, similar to the ones Steve used to wear on the Raised On Radio Tour with Journey, was lowered from the rafters right above the stage. Steve would turn over in surprise and then he'd start walking around it looking intrigued; finally he'd grab the microphone and he would start an amusing "conversation" with the tailed coat: *"I heard a rumor you retired...I heard a rumor you had lost your voice. Well, you don't look bad for all the miles you have on you!"* Then he would say, undecided: *" I don't know...Maybe we'll leave it up to them...What do you people think?"* Steve would turn to his audience who would start cheering loudly, so the next thing was Steve pulling off the tux from its hanger, put it on and start singing "Lovin`, Touchin` , Squeezin`". It was a completely delightful, funny moment which the fans enjoyed so much that Steve decided to play this little part in every show throughout the tour!

The overall concept of the Strange Medicine Tour was something that Steve wanted to do for a long time. His affection for the fans and the joy of meeting them again made him wish for a closer relationship with the people in the audience. His philosophy was simple: *"When we were playing big arenas, most people walked out of there feeling an intimacy anyway - at least that's what I tried to put across. I was raised to believe that you are supposed to go out there and perform, interact, communicate and enjoy. The audience enjoys the performance and you enjoy them enjoying the performance and it goes back and forth. Everybody shares a great moment, all together."*

Steve chose to put up the shows in smaller venues and the best idea was to sing in restored theaters all over America. He would say: *"Every time I'd do a sound check I would feel so special to be in those theaters."* All along the tour, Steve enjoyed an amazing intimacy with the audience - it was a warm closeness shared through music and emotion. When asked later about the reason why there aren't any filmed shows from the 1994 Tour, Steve admitted that he decided not to tape any of the concerts. The reason was he and his band wanted to feel comfortable on stage and really have fun without worrying about cameras all over the place. Every night, Steve was putting together a vibrant show that would take the audience on cloud nine; people were rediscovering the same passionate singer and entertainer just as he was during the Journey years and the familiar sound of those beautiful songs was getting straight to their hearts. Then it was Steve`s new music that revealed an intense part of his artistic creativity and a much more passionate vocal approach – his musical force was a fascinating thing to experience in a live circumstance.

The Strange Medicine Band that was going with Steve on the road was slightly different from the one that he had worked with in the studio, meaning that the new bass player was Todd Jensen, a musician who had played previously in the rock group Hardline. Jensen was a great addition to the tour formula and more, he was feeling great to be a part of Steve's solo project because, he confessed, *"I'm in a comfort zone being in Steve's band because of his R'n'B roots"*. The most important thing was that Steve was getting along with his musicians extremely well – they were clicking together on stage and they were also getting along great off stage. During the first months of the Strange Medicine Tour they already had a great friendship going on and everytime they went up on stage they were putting up some dazzling shows in all those intimate venues, just like they were throwing a big private party for friends – it was a wonderful feeling that impressed the audiences everywhere.

Steve was a veteran tour musician – while being on the road he was taking care of his voice and his physical condition by following the same strict routine he was already used to from his endless Journey tours; he also had all kinds of preparation habits before every show. For example, Moyes Lucas remembers how everyone got to know what made Steve get in the mood before a concert: *"Every night before Steve was getting ready to go onstage he would be listening to Sam Cooke records. You would come in and hear those Sam Cooke records and you'd know Steve was there getting ready for the show."* Then Steve would call his band for the vocal warm up session before going on stage; usually they would do their voice warm ups in the bathrooms because the acoustics were just great in there and the vocal harmonies sounded good – Steve had a good vocal warm up with his band before every single show.

The tour covered the US from East to West, but traveling from venue to venue was pleasurable as they would all have a lot of fun in the tour bus which was driven by Frank – in fact the bus was called "Frank's Rolling Dinner" and it was a great cozy place for sleeping, eating and having some good laughs!

On the 22nd of January 1995, the Strange Medicine Tour arrived in Columbus, Ohio. It was Steve's 46th Birthday and that night he was getting ready for a show at the Veterans Memorial. There were a lot of surprises on the way for Steve and the first one came right from his band – they put together a backstage celebration with a beautiful white cake decorated with chocolate musical notes, champagne and lots of funny snap shots! Steve was very touched and happy to share that special day with his friends. However, the best was yet to come that same night, during the concert. At one point before a song, Steve's band mates looked at each other and they started playing and singing the traditional *"Happy Birthday"* tune, only this time it had a good guitar riff to it and it was sung *" to Stephen"*! All of a sudden, the entire audience began singing along – it was amazing! Steve's surprise was huge and he started laughing while looking at his friends on stage; then he turned to the people in the crowd and he said: *"Thank you for sharing my 39th Birthday with me!"* Everyone laughed and cheered loudly, then Steve paused – he extremely touched by all this. The love he was getting from all those people around him was unbelievable. He took a deep breath trying to control his voice as he was getting too emotional. *"Oh...You know, I never used to work on my Birthday but tonight we are here in your town...It's been eight years since I've had the opportunity to sing for you people...you know what I'm sayin'?...So...I want to dedicate this next song to the person who brought me into this life...and I'll sing it for her and I'll sing it for you because you are the faithful ones..."* "Faithfully" started playing and the place went wild. It was not only one of the most beloved songs from the Journey era, but it has been Steve's mother's favorite songs of all – that made the moment even more poignant. Steve would always remember his mother especially on his Birthday and now he was singing that song just like she was there. That special night in Columbus was one that Steve never forgot.

*

During the Medicine Tour, Steve was constantly invited to do radio interviews and usually, during the shows, they were taking calls from the fans who wanted to ask him questions. One of these radio shows turned out to be a little different. Steve's tour reached the city of Wheeling, West Virginia, and he was invited to be on-air at 107.5 The Eagle's Morning Show. As calls started to come in, a man got on air and said he wanted to apologize to Steve. When Steve asked him amused what was the reason, the man said that in 1986, during a concert in Greensboro...he was the one who threw that watch towards Steve and injured his eye! Steve was completely stunned! He couldn't believe he was talking to this man who said he waited all these years only to have the chance to apologize! It was such an emotional moment for Steve – he accepted the man's apologies, then he asked for his phone number and promised him he would call him back after the radio show was done. Then Steve confessed to the listeners that throughout the years he sometimes thought about that Greensboro incident, although he never kept the anger as he knew the man didn't really mean to do what he did. Nonetheless, it was so strange that everything came in full circle after seven years!

In the following couple of months, the Strange Medicine Tour covered most of the North American continent. Starting the 10th of March 1995, a new opening band joined Steve on the road, an eclectic acoustic stomp band named Bonepony. They played as an opening act until the middle of March, when Steve went to sing in Fresno. He had a lot of memories related to this city which he loved; last time he performed there was with Journey. He remembered that benefit concert for the Valley Children's Hospital from 1983, the great times they all had back then and he felt nostalgic remembering the good old rock'n'roll days. Returning to Fresno was very special as this time he played at the Warners Theater - Steve was absolutely savoring the positive feeling he'd get in that cozy venue filled with cheerful people.

This tour was set to be a full-scale success. Steve and the Strange Medicine Band played sold out concerts everywhere they went and the response of the critics was absolutely great. Steve Perry was a household name and his unmatched talent was awe-inspiring for everyone. But the most pleasurable moments were those when Steve would meet his fans. In the past, he confessed he worried about getting in the middle of a large number of fans to sign autographs or talk, but not because he didn't enjoy spending time with people but because he would take great risks – he stated once that it would be enough that one of the fans had the flu and he would have been in danger of getting it too. That would've jeopardized his health and voice and he couldn't afford getting sick, especially back then in the heavy touring situation with Journey, when he had to sing every single night. But this time, during the Strange Medicine Tour, he was much more relaxed and he didn't care. He was missing his fans so much that he agreed to come and meet them in special places; the Steve Perry Information Network, supervised by Lora Beard and Cynthia Poon, was arranging these meet and greet sessions – it was an excellent system for the admirers to get close to their idol and a wonderful way for Steve to get in touch with all those who have been faithful fans all through the years. Maybe it was because of the crowded places, maybe it was the change of season but anyway, by the end of March, Steve began feeling sick. At first he thought it was a minor treatable flu but unfortunately things were far from being ok – he got more and more weak and the doctors confirmed what he feared most: he had contracted a severe form of bronchitis which needed immediate care and total rest. On the 22nd of March, the Strange Medicine Tour ended in San Juan, Puerto Rico and right after that Steve was hospitalized for intensive treatment – he spent a couple of weeks fighting high fever and trying to recover from the physical weakness. His band mates were concerned about his condition but they knew Steve is going to get well because he was in good hands. However, while his body was getting better, something unexpected was happening to Steve at an emotional level. During his recovery he had time to think about the tour he just had to cancel; the fact that he was back in the music business, experiencing again the pleasure of singing, the thrill of being received with so much love by the fans – all those things brought up feelings that he thought he'd buried a long time ago. He was longing for something he once possessed, something that was a part of his life no matter how much things changed throughout the years.

Soon, Steve had to be honest with him: he was missing Journey.

Jars Of Clay

"But we have this treasure in jars of clay to show that this all-surpassing power is from God and not from us. We are hard pressed on every side, but not crushed; perplexed, but not in despair; persecuted, but not abandoned; struck down, but not destroyed."

2nd Book of Corinthians, Chapter 4 Verses 7-9

It all started with a phone call and it almost felt like suddenly reconnecting with a past life. After a few seconds, Jon Cain answered. The surprise of hearing Steve's voice on the line was so unexpected that he didn't know what to say for a few moments. Steve confessed later: *"I was excited his number hadn't changed...I hadn't talked to him in years."* It was true, the two of them didn't keep in touch for quite some time although Jon has been aware of Steve's return to the music business. More, Jon kept hoping that somehow, someway Journey will be back again just like before the 1987 split. His hopes got even higher after he heard "Anyway" - Steve's song from the "For The Love Of Strange Medicine" album. Cain publicly stated that after hearing that song he felt that Steve was healing and that maybe they would have a chance to get back together. And now, out of the blue, Steve was calling him.

It was the summer of 1995, a few months after Steve cancelled the Strange Medicine Tour because of his severe health problems. But now he was completely recovered and the desire of getting back with Journey was just consuming. He confessed in an interview at the time: *"Underneath it all, I was missing more and more being the singer in Journey than I ever thought I would."* Then he added in all sincerity: *"You start to recognize that some of the things you didn't even know you had as a group in the music are still there and you've been looking for them in a long time. All you have to do is put your guns down and get back together again."* Steve admitted:*" Individually, none of us made the magic as magically as we collectively make it together."*

Talking with Jon brought back a lot of memories – it seemed like they have never been apart. Yet, Steve felt that Jon was intrigued by his phone call so he told him they should get together and have an honest talk. Then Steve said to Jonathan: *"It's been many years...and I got this yearning to be in Journey again."*

After talking to Jon Cain, Steve spoke to Neal Schon too and all three of them decided to meet face to face and find out if they could pick up things where they left them. They met in Sausalito, California, the same small town where Raised On Radio was recorded almost ten years before. Steve remembers what he said to Jon there, in that coffee shop where they met: *"Just listen, before it's too late. For reasons God only knows, there's a lot of people out there who love us, and I saw some of them not too long ago. Maybe it's time to try again."* They talked about a lot of things and straightening everything out between them was the most important step before talking about Journey's future. Slowly they realized that not many things have changed over the years – they sure had the same passion for music, especially if it was about Journey's music. They took some decisions that day and put together a plan for a special Journey comeback. That included bringing back two of the old Journey members: Ross Valory and Steve Smith. This was going to be a golden line-up reunion.

But before starting to work on music together, the band had to find the perfect manager who was supposed to handle the huge mission of bringing back the most acclaimed AOR band. Everything had to be perfect. They decided to let go of Herbie Herbert's management services and start fresh with someone else from the industry. It wasn't easy to change the manager considering that Herbert had been the father figure of the band for so many years. Steve commented later: *"I think that Herbie and I are similar in a lot of areas; I think he likes to feel that he has as much autonomy to decide things...I think I do too, and more so maybe than the rest of the members"*. Herbert agreed to let the band go so now all the Journey members were ready to give a shot to a few experienced managers. In the Fall on 1995, the band started interviewing some of the best names in the business. It was a hard task to find the perfect guy for this enterprise – he wasn't supposed to have only great managerial skills but he also had to believe in the Journey concept. Throughout this search, Steve remembers an episode that made him realize the importance of the unity of a band. *"There was a guy named Marty, a brilliant man, and he was one of the possible managers, and he turned to us one day and just looked us straight in the eye and said "No matter what you do, there's just no reason to attack the group. And I mean, don't attack it from within, and don't attack yourselves". And it was kinda like a reverent statement and I took it to heart."* After meeting several managers, Steve and his band mates decided to stop and hire Irving Azoff. Azoff was a major name in the music industry and he had been known for taking care of the career and the comeback of The Eagles – he was the perfect choice. But Steve admitted that Irving was chosen for an obvious reason: *"He's done an incredible job with the Eagles, but that didn't have a lot to do with why we picked him. It was more because we all felt overwhelmingly comfortable about working with him."* Irving Azoff was excited to take over the management helm as he stated later: *"I felt that Journey was a unique missed opportunity, a band that had a legion of fans out there willing to participate in again."*

The news of Journey reuniting with Steve Perry as the front man again set the music world on fire. Some didn't even believe it was happening for real until the official press release announced their comeback. The fans were simply ecstatic. What they had hoped for and dreamed of for almost a decade was finally coming true. Journey was back in the same exquisite line-up that conquered the world and they were ready to reward their faithful fans with the magic of their music. Just like expected, everybody was eager to find out all the details of Journey's unforeseen reunion – the "when"-s, "why"-s and "how"-s were aiming especially Steve, so he and the band released some statements and gave some interviews to provide the details people wanted to know. Therefore, Lora Beard returned to her task of delivering Journey's official messages to the fans through a special Hotline. When Steve was asked about how he feels about picking up the Journey act just where he left it, he declared in all honesty: *"I don't know if I want to pick up where I left off. The music business can be a choke chain, and you have to be aware of that, especially when you still have a few marks around your neck from it."*

All this time Steve was thinking about the music he wanted to do. He was anxious to start writing Journey songs again – it was all about that artistic vibration he'd been missing for so long. *"I really missed working with Neal and Jon"*, he confessed, *"and the kind of energy that happens between us musically and the songwriting process, the recording process…You know, it brings a certain kind of voice outta me that I can't get anywhere"*. Steve was convinced that if the new songs will come together as honestly as they have always been, then they will have a good reason to make a true Journey album. He stated: *"We didn't want to resurrect a dream just to put it on life support."*

*

In the first months of 1996, Steve, Neal and Jon started working on the brand new songs that were going to make Journey's reunion album. Usually, they would meet over at Jon Cain's house near San Francisco and work together on the ideas they had. They were amazed of how naturally they clicked again, it was like they haven't been apart for nine years – that beautiful magic feeling was there again and it was as powerful as always. *"That was the first thing we had to do - see if we had the spark to write again"*, Steve said. *"The big exciting thing was when we really got back into the song writing process; it was kinda scary how the songs came quick. It really proved to us once again maybe something we forgot, that there was an awful lot of chemistry there."*

All the songs they wrote then had a depth they never had before – it was just as all that time they've been separated helped them mature artistically; the lyrics had meaningful messages and the music had an emotional pulse to it. Steve was convinced that the special Journey sound was going to be greater that ever. *"Everything had to have happened as it did"*, he said, *"You can't push the river any quicker than it flows."*

One of the new songs had a special meaning to Steve – it was a beautiful ballad that was destined to become one of the best songs in the band's career. In one of his interviews at the time, Steve recalled the way that song was put together: *"I was driving on the freeway going to Jonathan's house and Neal was there waiting and we were doing our writing sessions. And I have a mini cassette player that I keep with me all the time and, out of the blue, the chorus of 'When You Love A Woman' came into my mind and I sang the whole chorus into the box then got there and then we quickly finished it"*. Another very special song that was going to be one of the stirring ballads on the new album was named "When I Think Of You". For many years after the album was out, no one knew what has been the source of inspiration behind that tune, but Steve revealed all that in one of his recent Fan Asylum interviews: *"It's about a dream I had... I had this dream that Mom was working in this really cool gift shop with cobalt colored crystal and when I walked into the shop, Mom was standing in the distance with her back to me. She slowly turned around and smiled at me. In my dream I started to cry because she looked so good, not as I last remembered her. Then I saw her fearless comforting eyes and I could feel she was happy."*

The song that gave the album title, "Trial By Fire", was perhaps the most meaningful track of all. Steve recalled how he showed up at rehearsal one day and Neal was already there playing this great line on his guitar. They started working on it right away and before they knew it the song was finished. Steve was impressed by its message: *"That song and the lyrics to that song helped me during the writing of it but also after the album was done. It actually gave me strength to deal with what was going on around me... 'It's just another trial by fire'"*.

At the beginning of May 1996 the entire band was ready to start the studio work. With Kevin Shirley taking care of the production part, Journey went into of the most advanced studios on the West Coast: The Site at Skywalker Ranch Studios. Skywalker Ranch was the headquarters of Lucasfilm and it was a fabulous place located in Marin County, California, 45 minutes north of San Francisco. The Site was a state-of-the-art studio, fully equipped with everything Journey needed for a special sounding album. Steve prepared himself up for a meticulous recording session – the music was thought provoking and the feel of the entire album was based on a melodious sound beautifully carried out by everyone in the band. There was a spiritual perception that animated the entire creative process and this was sure going to be a mature album meant to express a considerable range of feelings and tones. Steve`s voice sounded hauntingly beautiful on each and every track and his delivery was absolutely breathtaking. He was pouring his soul into each song and the results were fantastic. They entire band spent four months at The Site and there was a great deal of work involved. There was harmony between them, but there were arguments too, as Steve stated in an interview at the time: *"We didn't know if we'd get the studio and chew each other's faces off or be grateful to be back together. There were some clashes. Democracy is a nice concept, but it doesn't work easily in rock bands."* Sometimes, fatigue was taking a toll on Steve but he was getting back on track everytime as this was an album fit for his musical sensitivity and he was absolutely determined to focus and make the best of it. "When You Love A Woman" was the first track cut on the new CD and the band chose the final form of the song on the third or fourth take. They were playing live, Steve sang live, and there were hardly any overdubs at all.

Finally, by the end of July, Journey had already recorded all the songs and they were going through the painstaking mixing process which took almost a month – at the end of August 1996, they announced that the "Trial By Fire" album was done. The new record had fifteen remarkable musical gems that compiled the entire creativity of five exceptional musicians.

Now it was time for Journey to get out of the studio and get ready for the reunion tour. The album had to be taken out on the road and presented to the millions of ardent fans.

*

On a very hot summer day, in the beautiful island of Maui, Hawaii, Steve Perry was hiking on a steep mountain. He was alone, just like he preferred everytime he was training. He knew the places well as it wasn't the first time he was doing this to get in shape for an upcoming tour. It was his favorite location for gearing up because the mountain was very demanding on his body – but that was exactly what he needed to get in the best physical condition necessary for a long tour. At one point he felt that the heat was almost unbearable and he had been straining himself too much so he decided to quit the workout for that day. Steve started rapidly descending the mountain, maybe a little too fast; suddenly he felt a flash of devastating pain in his left hip. It was so intense it took his breath away. He stopped trying to regain his balance and he looked around confused. He tried to stay calm and figure out what was going on, but he couldn't understand - the pain was just there. He tried to walk again but the twinge wouldn't go away – it was burning his left side with intensity. Steve didn't know what to believe. He was healthy, his body was in excellent shape and he never had any problems like this before. Fighting with the severe ache, he managed to get off the mountain and first thing when he got back to the hotel was to call Journey's manager, Irving Azoff, telling him that something was wrong with his hip, that he never felt such an excruciating pain in his life before and that he's going to take the first flight back to Los Angeles.

After getting back home, Steve remembers: *"I started a series of doctors to check out what is going on because I was never in this kind of pain."* After a few weeks the terrible truth came out: Steve was diagnosed with a form of degenerative bone disease. All the doctors were telling him the same thing: the only way to permanently solve the problem was to get a hip replacement surgery.

Steve went through a succession of detailed medical tests in order to find an alternative solution for this crisis. He just couldn't decide to have a hip surgery and his hope was to find another way to cure the disease. He was going through a lot of pain everyday but he tried to keep his faith and stay strong because he had a mission with Journey. In the meantime, things were moving fast for the band. The "Trial by Fire" album was ready to be released in November and in between medical tests, Steve had to do interviews, photo sessions and promotional work. In November of 1996 the new album went straight to the number three position in the US charts and started selling like gold. The first single "When You Love A Woman" was taking everyone's breath away - it was such a brilliant ballad that it is considered to this day one of the most exquisitely structured rock ballads in the world. In January of

1997, the song was nominated in the category for 'Best Pop Performance by a Duo or Group with Vocal' for the 39th Annual Grammy Awards. Unfortunately, Journey lost to Beatles. But the radio stations all over America were playing "When you Love A Woman" in heavy rotation. Rob Roberts, PD at Miami Top 40 station WHYI said: *"We got a copy of the song a few days early and just threw it on the air. I went bananas when I heard it. This song is huge; this is a monster".* Journey was riding the high waves of success again and Steve was completely overwhelmed, as he said when he found out about the nomination: *"After being gone we came back with a song that was nominated for Grammy. You don't know what that meant to us. It meant that what we did is not gonna be a hack thing".*

"When You Love A Woman" was destined to be more than a top song – this beautiful ballad was going to have one of the classiest videos in Journey's career. On the 2nd of December 1996, the entire band went back to Marin County to start working on the video for the song. The location was again the Skywalker Ranch Studios, there were they recorded the Trial By Fire album. But this time Steve and his band mates were going to work in the ideal setting for the video as the Skywalker Ranch had one of the most impressive scoring stages in the West. The main room, measuring sixty feet by eighty feet long with a thirty foot ceiling, had enough space for a one hundred and twenty five piece symphony orchestra. It was a magnificent place equipped with a state-of-the –art adjustable acoustic system. That day, all the musical instruments were brought in and set in place. The director of the video, Wayne Isham, took care of the mini-orchestra that was going to accompany the Journeymen all through the song. Steve was getting ready for some long hours of filming and he wasn't feeling too well because the pain in his left hip was starting to get a bit too strong. The actual shooting of the various parts of the video was a demanding task – Steve was is deep pain and no matter how much he struggled with the ache, he still had to stop from time to time. It was too much. He confessed later: *"In between takes, I would literally walk with a cane, hobble over to a little private room where I could pack the front and the back of my left side of the body with ice; then I would wait for the next camera shot to be set up then go out there and do it."* Finally, everything was over and Steve was thankful that he could take a break and rest. More than that, he realized that he had to do something soon to get out of this situation. He was still undecided about what he should do - avoiding the surgery would've meant more pain and time was definitely working against him. Because of his condition he couldn't be present at too many promotional events like before because he was afraid he would not pass the test. *"The camera was going to 'see' my pain",* Steve said *,"the microphone will 'hear' that I'm in pain".*

Now the main concern was the upcoming tour that was planed for the next year. People were anxiously waiting to see their rock idols getting up on stage together after almost a decade of absence. The pressure and the anticipation were growing day by day. Steve was caught between a rock and a hard place – he wanted to go out there and do what he wanted to do for so long, but in the same time he was dealing with the personal health decisions he had to make sooner or later. He admitted in a later statement: *"I was faced with 'do I take care of myself and do things as I possibly can or I just throw myself in the situation and do it even if I'm not ready to do it'?"*

The Christmas of 1997 was very agitated for Steve, Neal and Jonathan. All three of them were constantly trying to answer the huge number of questions coming from the fans. People were already aware of the fact that Steve was having some health issues, but he wasn't too comfortable talking about that. He was the same private, media shy person as always but he tried to open up to the fans as much as he could.

Journey's comeback was a huge event, the album was selling massively all over the world and the Trial By Fire Tour was already discussed for the summer of 1998. But Steve wasn't doing well at all. The medication and the treatment he was getting wasn't improving his health condition and the beginning of 1998 found him seriously doubting that he could put up with the rigors of a long tour. He was constantly looking for alternatives to patch up his hip condition but the only valid answer he was getting was leading him to the same conclusion: sooner or later he was going to have to consider a hip surgery.

*

Just like in 1995 Steve called Jonathan Cain for a new start, now, in January of 1998, it was Jon's turn to make a phone call to Steve. This time is was the beginning of the end. The whole situation was already under considerable pressure: Journey needed an extensive summer tour in order to promote the "Trial By Fire" album but they couldn't do anything as long as Steve's health was getting critical. Steve's band mates were losing their patience. They were frustrated and nervous as they knew they had to make a decision about the future things to come. Steve had numerous talks with them and his colleagues were willing to wait for him to recover but only under one condition: that he would take the surgery immediately. But Steve just couldn't rush this and he was reluctant – the decision was a very stressful process as it was about his life and his well being. He stated at the time:*" I understand this frustration of wanting to get out on tour, because I was also very upset and frustrated. But I just didn't feel like being hooked up to a mule team after surgery…It was kind of an ultimatum. I said, 'hopefully, you're going to do what's right for you, and I guess I'm doing what's right for me.'"*

The other members of Journey decided it would be better if they would try to move on and find a replacement for Steve Perry as long as his health problems were going to take some time to be fixed and therefore will sideline him for some time. But it wasn't easy to take such a decision. They knew Steve Perry was Journey's icon and it was hard to think about anyone else taking his place as a front man.

In the meantime, it was Jonathan's task to call Steve and tell him about the band's decision. Steve remembers that call and all the strange feelings he was experiencing; in an afterward interview he revealed what he said to Jon Cain that day. He asked the band to reconsider and have patience with the whole situation until he gets his health back. But the most painful part for Steve was he felt the Journey legacy was going to be harmed. He asked Jon not to break the name of Journey: *"Don't crack the stone. Go out there and do whatever you want to, with whomever you want to and call it whatever you want to, but leave Journey alone"*. But Jonathan Cain told him that they had already decided to move on and do everything under the name of Journey with a new lead singer. Steve knew that if they would do that there will be no turning back for him and the band. He told that to Jon and Jon said: *"I know that."* It was a tough moment. All the magic they had, all the dreams they shared together as a band – everything was gone.

On the 8th of May, 1998, Journey officially announced that Steve Perry was no longer the lead singer of Journey.

The curtain fell for the last time.

Standing Alone

The symphony orchestra was playing along with Steve Perry, as he was standing in the middle of this huge studio. The cameras were rolling and behind Steve there was a giant movie screen which was showing scenes from the newest Warner Brothers animation musical movie "Quest for Camelot". The song, written by David Foster, Carole Bayer Sager and Steve Perry, was called "I Stand Alone" and it had a powerful message, both in melody and words; all this was enriched by the addition of a full orchestra and Steve's exquisite voice. Back in 1984 Steve was talking about his greatest fantasy: *"After singing rock for so many years I'd give anything to sing with a symphony orchestra"*. Finally, after almost fifteen years his dream came true.

Steve was approached by David Foster and asked to record two songs, "I Stand Alone" and "United We Stand", that were going to be included on the soundtrack of the Warner Brothers animated movie. Steve was still struggling with his health problems, but he was thrilled by the opportunity to record a song that had a special ring to it, so he took the offer. In May of 1998, the animated movie was released in theaters across America, along with the video for "I Stand Alone". Steve was invited to the premiere and he agreed to make a brief appearance. Although his projects and his ideas kept him pretty busy, it wasn't easy for him to get through the tough times after he had to leave Journey. But Steve was decided not to look back, take each day at a time and do what he was supposed to do at his own pace.

The summer of 1998 found Steve putting together a solo album as he decided to release a collection of his solo work which was going to be named "Greatest Hits + 5 Unreleased". This album was going to include some of the songs from Steve's first solo album "Street Talk" from 1984, a few songs from his 1994 album "For The Love Of Strange Medicine" as well as some unreleased tracks from the abandoned "Against The Wall" album. He explained: *"The ('Against The Wall') album was recorded right after the 'Street Talk' record and it was due to be released. But then I went back to Journey and went on tour. And it sort of got shelved in the can"*. However, the biggest surprise was that Steve added on the Greatest Hits +5 album the demo song that got him to be the lead singer of Journey: "If You Need Me Call Me". This was the same tune that Herbie Herbert had listened to on that day back in the summer of 1977 and made him decide to bring Steve into the band. All in all, Steve was very pleased about the outcome of his project. *"The songs are exactly the way I envisioned them"*, he said, *" They sound as good to me today as they did then."* Some of the songs that were never released before had a special recording story behind them. In one of his later interviews, Steve shared the way "Melody" and "When You`re In Love For The First Time" were done: *"It happens from time to time when you first write a song and you have a piece of tape sitting there, and you`re going to try the lyrics that you just finished and sing the song for the first time ...usually, you can't beat that moment... That`s great. It can happen just like that."*.

Although this project kept his mind busy, Steve`s main concern was his health. While working on his Greatest Hits album, Steve had to finally make a decision: he was going to have the hip replacement surgery in October of 1998.The therapy wasn't working, so that was the only way to get well.

*

It was a new millennium. It felt just like starting to live all over again.

That was Steve Perry's sensation after getting over the hip replacement surgery and the recovery process. He left everything behind and thought about living life under his own terms. He didn't stop writing songs and sketching projects, but he decided to take it easy and enjoy everyday life much more than he did before. *"I have a private side of my life. I like to keep a piece of Steve's soul for himself"*. In all honesty, Steve shared his new state of mind with his fans in one of his latest interviews: *"I'm on this side of the looking glass for a change. I've been letting people entertain me. I never took the time to let someone entertain me before. I was always the one doing the entertaining. My life has kind of turned around to where I've been able to take advantage of my time right now."*

Although his private life was keeping him away from the fuss of the music industry, Steve was constantly approached by other musicians to collaborate on different projects, but he just couldn't honor them all; however, he was excited to visit some fellow musicians and watch their recording sessions – this part of the creation process was still a favorite thing of his. That's how Steve ended up being a vocal guest on guitarist Jeff Golubs's album "Soul Sessions". In 2003 Steve was in Los Angeles and he stopped by the studio to say hello to an old friend of his, drummer Steve Ferrone, and the next thing was that Jeff invited Steve to lend his voice to one of the songs named "Can't Let You Go". Golub told the story: *"We all thought it was pretty cool just to have the singer from "Journey" at the studio. We were recording a ballad that I had written and during a play back Steve says to me 'Man, I could really here this vocal line going along with your guitar'. Of course I had the engineer set up a microphone immediately and the next thing you know, I've got Steve Perry singing on my record!!! How cool is that!!".* Still, the most unexpected project in Steve's career was yet to come. In that same year of 2003, he received a very sincere letter from Oscar winner actress Charlize Theron. She was very excited about this movie she was working on with her good friend, director Patty Jenkins. It was a real story about the life of Aileen Wuornos, one of America's first female serial killers. One of the key scenes in the movie required a special song and Patty Jenkins decided she wanted to use Journey's hit from 1982 "Don't Stop Believin'". Steve was impressed: *"I was moved by the letter and I returned the phone call, talked to Charlize for a while, and then Patty came on and we talked for a long time, and they said 'could we just send you a piece of the film so you can see what we're talking about?' So they sent me a piece of the film".* After watching the clip, Steve was impressed: *"It was the first time I'd seen almost a literal translation. So I called back and said 'could I come down and, you know, meet you, and talk to you guys about it?'."* Charlize Theron was excited: *"Steve just really got into the story",* she said, *" He flew from San Francisco to L.A. and ended up spending two months with us during postproduction. It was like we were in a band with Steve Perry!"*

"Monster" came out in 2003 and it was a huge box-office success as well as an Oscar winner in 2004. More so, Steve was credited as a Music Consultant for his great input in the production process. *"I really enjoyed participating in this side of the project.",* Steve confessed. *"Later Patty and B.T. insisted on me giving me Music Consultant credit. I was stunned".*

But that wasn't the only project Steve had been working on that year. In the summer of 2003 he got a proposition from John Kalodner, the legendary A&R man, who asked Steve to oversee some of Journey's video footage throughout the years. The idea was to put together all that video footage on a special DVD for all the fans to enjoy the band's outstanding work throughout the years. *"Immediately, I thought this was an amazing idea,"* Steve said, *" but there would be logistical problems to overcome. Though the visuals are great, the audio of today has far surpassed the original sound on those tapes. All the tracks have been digitally remastered."*

In November of 2003 the Greatest Hits 1978 – 1997 DVD was released and had eighteen videos of Journey from the time the band was fronted by Steve Perry – it was a fascinating voyage into the history of one of the greatest AOR bands in the world. As a reaction, the fans were hoping that Steve, along with John Kalodner, would consider releasing more DVDs with footage from the past. Soon enough, their wishes were granted: in 2005, Steve produced a second DVD – this time it was the full length Escape Tour concert filmed by MTV on the 6th of November 1981 at the Houston Summit in Texas. He decided to bring back to life their stellar performance from that day, and that meant some really hard technical work: Steve worked on the project in a studio in Los Angeles, remastering and remixing the original MTV tapes. Spending up to fourteen hours in the studio everyday and having to watch every second of the performance as it was, got Steve through an overabundance of feelings that took him back to the most wonderful times he had with Journey. He sincerely admitted in one of his recent interviews that it was painful looking back on the time he and Journey shared together: *"I sat in the studio for six weeks with this DVD mixing it in stereo then tore in down and mixed in 5.1... that was one of the best pleasures I've had other than the emotional aspect of being dragged through the plethora of emotions from 'what happened' to 'we were great' to 'look how young we were' and remembering all the stupid things we were doing to each other when we didn't know what we had."*

Although Steve was still staying away from the limelight, his fame was keeping him in everyone's attention. Because of his recent production work, the fans were hoping for a full return into the music business, but Steve was not quite willing to do that. He preferred to avoid the industry's merry-go-round and do things at his own tempo. Still, he was willing to work on some projects, especially if he believed in their quality. That's how he accepted an invitation coming from David Pack, the ex-lead singer of the band Ambrosia. David and Steve were long time friends and David's request for Steve to participate as a vocal guest on his upcoming album was a very nice surprise. When the project was in the works, Steve went down to Burbank, California to be a part of the recording sessions. Their collaboration became a very fruitful one: not only Steve recorded the vocals for the song "A Brand New Start" but he also co-produced it. His duet with David Pack turned out to be awesome – their voices worked great together and the track was destined to be one of the best from the album. David Pack confessed: *"Steve is one of my favorite people on the planet...amazing person, amazing writing intuition, amazing voice...he's the best, and we truly enjoy working together"*. Pack's album was released the next year and besides Steve Perry it had other famous guest stars as well: Ann Wilson from Heart, Dewey Bunnell from America and Timothy B. Schmit from The Eagles.

The end of 2005 found Steve satisfied with everything he had accomplished, as both David Pack's album and the "Live In Houston 1981" DVD were successfully released.

After he completed all these projects, Steve went back enjoying his private life, but soon he heard the news: after twenty-two years since they have been nominated, Journey was finally going to receive a Star on the famous Hollywood Walk of Fame. The date set for the event was the 21st of January 2005.

*

The bright Southern California sun was shining that Friday of January 2005, warming up the streets of Hollywood. Tinsel Town was flooded by the large number of people who were coming in the city from all over the United States and the world. It was a special day which was meant to honor the career and the success of one of the most beloved AOR bands in the world: Journey.

This was the talk of the town and everywhere you'd turn you would see happy faces and impatient fans; many people were carrying old vinyl Journey albums, CDs, vintage posters or wearing those unforgettable Journey t-shirts. The pride of being a Journey fan was obviously shown by each and every one of them. At every corner you could hear lively conversations about Journey's music, people were sharing dear concert memories but most of all, everybody was eagerly waiting the ceremony of unveiling the Journey Star. The event was set to start at 11:30 a.m. in front of the Musician's Institute at 6750 Hollywood Boulevard. An excited crowd gathered around the hot spot of the day and got ready to greet the members of the band who were expected to arrive any minute now. It was going to be a fantastic meeting between the fans and all the past and present members of Journey who were invited to honor the event with their presence.

All over the Hollywood Boulevard you could hear the sound of the classic Journey songs and all those beautiful tunes made people nostalgic, as Steve Perry's unmistakable voice filled the air. As the time for the festivities was getting closer, everyone was asking the same question: "Will Steve Perry show up?". Since the day it was announced that Journey will receive a Star on the Walk Of Fame rumors never ceased flying around. The presence of Steve was still uncertain, even then, minutes away from the ceremony. No one knew anything for sure. Johnny Grant, the Mayor of Hollywood, started checking the microphones on the podium. The big moment was almost there.

Suddenly, all eyes turned to the VIP gate of the Musician's Institute and as the gate opened…Steve Perry himself walked through smiling and waving to all those people who at first were in deep shock – most of them had lost the hope of seeing Steve there and the surprise of his appearance was more than words could express. For a few seconds there was silence and then the crowd started screaming and clapping hands. Their happiness was breathtaking! Some of the people started crying, others were yelling out Steve`s name, cameras were flashing incessantly – this encounter between him and the fans was truly magical. Steve confessed later: *"The fans energy was something I had not felt in a long time. I get high just thinking about it!"* After a few minutes the other members of Journey past and present walked through the gates: Neal Schon, Jonathan Cain, Ross Valory ,Deen Castronovo, Steve Augeri, Steve Smith, Aynsley Dunbar, Robert Fleischman and George Tickner were all there and soon the crowd was watching what they called "the most beautiful sight they have ever witnessed": all the Journey members were together again, shaking hands, hugging, laughing and talking to one another like they'd never been apart!

Steve was in a very emotional state of mind. He had been giving a lot of thinking about this event and for quite some time he just couldn't decide whether to go or not. A few months before the ceremony, he started feeling the pressure as everyone was asking him if he'd be joining his ex-colleagues at the ceremony. It was a tough decision to make mostly because of all the mixed feelings that have built up over the years. But finally, he thought it was best not to listen to anyone and take this decision all by himself. As the months passed he pondered and looked back reflecting on his career with Journey. So many great things were accomplished over the years, so many beautiful songs have reached into people's hearts, so much work and commitment was put into this band. Then one day, while having a peaceful vacation, Steve made his decision. He was sincere about what was going on in his mind at the time: *"It weighed on me heavy because I haven't been in the band since May of `98.And the thing that really, really kept on eating at me was that I got quiet one day in Hawaii and I asked myself what I should do. And then my mind said 'If your mom was alive, what would she tell you?'. And the answer really came. And the answer was 'Well, if anyone deserves to be there, I think you do.' And it wasn't that I was more deserving than anybody else, she was just simply saying that 'you deserve to be there as much as anybody else does'"*. He recalls the way he had to do things: *"I showed up. Walked out there, nobody knew. Not a person knew…I had to lie to everybody just so I could have the choice to choose!"*

That day of January 21st was set to become not only the greatest highlight in Journey's career, but it is also the official Journey Day in Hollywood as it was proclaimed so by the Mayor himself!

The podium next to the brand new Star was graced with the presence of a few Journey members and Ross Valory was the one who invited Steve up for a speech. Visibly moved by the way he was welcomed, Steve addressed the fans with affection: *"I had the most amazing pleasure to join a band that was already in existence with some of the finest musicians that were ever going on at that time. There was nobody better. Ainsley Dunbar was playing drums when I joined the band Ross Valory was playing bass, Greg Rolie was lead singer, keyboard player and Neal Schon was magic fingers guitar, and then it evolved and all of a sudden in came Steve Smith on drums extraordinaire, and Jon Cain, songwriter, singer, keyboardist, and "magic fingers" Neal Schon on guitar! So, I must say that I've had an extraordinary experience being in the band. It's been the most wonderful thing that ever happened to me and lastly, very lastly, I really mean this from the bottom of my heart..., you can have all the stuff that we knew it took, from management with a crew and the best players, but without you... you don't have s***! Ok, so this star really belongs to you and I wanna thank you for making it happen!"*

Steve left the podium obviously touched and so very happy about the emotional response of the fans. His heart was warmed up even more when he heard all those people singing out loud "Happy Birthday to you"…The next day Steve Perry was turning 56 and he had just received the best gift in his life: the Journey Star on the Hollywood Walk Of Fame!

*

"As crazy as it got, as insane as it got – it was MAGIC, and no one will be able to take away what was accomplished with this band." Steve also confessed he is thankful for all the wonderful times he had, for the opportunity to be able to share his music and his voice with all the people who loved him throughout his career. He was blessed to find the perfect band to fulfill his most precious dreams and looking back he felt proud to have done things with sheer passion.

"Journey was not just me. ", he said. *"Journey was an entity bigger than the pieces. It was the sum of the parts that made this bigger entity. When we were at our biggest peak there was such a lot of conversation at that point that groups didn't have too much identity which I found very, very disturbing because I've always felt and still do that Journey had its own identity. I would like to see it remembered for a group, the incarnation of myself and the guys as a group that had honest, honest heart-felt music. That really came from aggressive angst and passionate heart and all the stuff in between. "*

It was a wild and beautiful ride, a unique singer's journey – a singer born to bring the beauty of the Music into the world and also the living proof that dreams come true if you have faith.

Or, in the words of Steve Perry himself: *"If you've got something that you want to try and you believe in it, don't be afraid to run along and go for it. Go after it!"*

*****

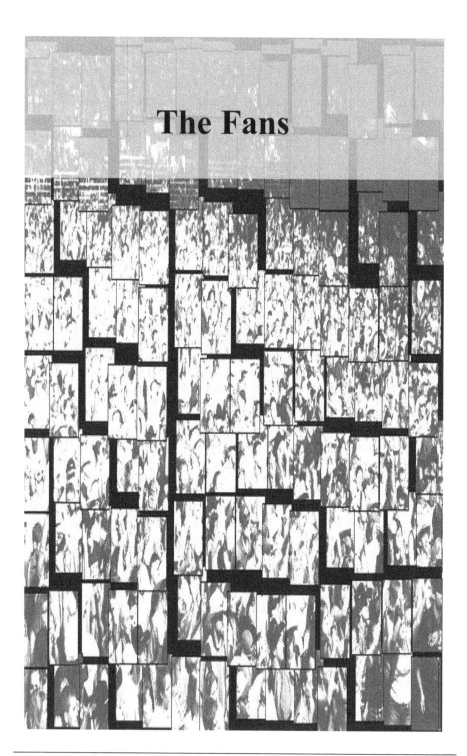

The Fans

Kay Marrone-Hansen

Sweet memory...... It was the long-awaited and so hoped-for 'Steve Perry Information Network (S.P.I.N.) Hometown Travel Package' - December 7-11, 1994 in San Francisco.

The first thing I want to say is that, as always, Lora Beard and Cyndy Poon (Fan Asylum) worked devotedly and tirelessly to put it together and make it work.......and in spite of the to-be-expected last minute glitches and panic-causing last second schedule changes in the rock world, they did an INCREDIBLE job! I'm forever grateful.

Just like all of you, I had waited and hoped for so long that Steve would be back. So when he did return (even without Journey and with the Strange Medicine band) it was a dream-come-true for me. I was ecstatic and emotional. I was crazy to see him and hear him whenever and wherever I possibly could. That was my agenda - period, whatever it took.

You see, I had never seen Journey LIVE...something I will always regret.....but at the time they were big and touring, I was all caught up and happily absorbed in being a new mommy...and besides, I figured they'd always be together. You know how that goes. So it was totally imperative for me to see Steve, because I felt in my heart he might not stay around all that long, and I was not going to miss him this time.

I wound up being blessed to see him 4 wonderful times during the short FTLOSM tour...at a private tour rehearsal at an L.A studio; in SF on our fan club trip; in L.A. at the Pantages (which I paid a small fortune for, to be able to stand at the edge of the stage! Worth every penny!); and in Santa Barbara. I also went on the Tahoe S.P.I.N. trip; however...that was the beginning of the end of the Strange Medicine band...and the tour. Steve got sick :(and there was no show. Shortly thereafter, S.P.I.N. also ended. The whole thing was so sad........but what an AWESOME several months it was while it lasted.

Ok...about the SF trip. I called Lora at the fan club A LOT, and even though I know I was making her crazy, she was always patient. She understood my need to 'be there' and see Steve. Then one day when I called her, she gave me the news I'd been hoping for......"Yes Kay, there's going to be a trip!" I won't even try to express my excitement......words would fall short! The fact that it was in SF made it that much sweeter...because of the whole Journey thing, AND because of the fact that although I'm a CA native, I had never been to the City by the Bay. I immediately made my flight arrangements, filled with indescribable joy!

Prior to the trip, I had had several shirts air-brushed....with Steve 'stuff'.... "PERRYlyzed!", "Have a Perry Christmas", "Somewhere There's Hope"....and a few more, each of which had various Steve things/musical notes, etc. airbrushed. The artist did an awesome job! They were all beautiful.

My flight was short and happy. I listened to Steve all the way there, and found myself thinking high school girl type thoughts about meeting him. I could tell you about everything I did and saw while in SF......(I love the city!!!!!); however, that's not what you want to hear about...so I'll get to the point.

On the day of our bus trip around SF, with plenty of pit and pic stops....it culminated at the Hard Rock Cafe for dinner. The whole group was in high spirits.....everyone just celebrating Steve's return to music. We were checking out the Journey stuff on the walls and just having a great time.

Suddenly an ecstatic, excited murmur goes through the crowd..."Oh my God!!!!! It's Steve!!!! Steve's here!!!!" was all you could hear. I turned around.........and there he was. I could not believe my eyes. My heart was pounding so loud, I swear you could hear it over the noise in there!!! Steve had come to see us at the Hard Rock Cafe!!!!! No one expected it, and I can't even begin to express what it felt like to see him............but just let your minds go there....and you'll know.

Well, he went to every one of our tables, sat down, and just chatted like an old and dear friend with every single one of us! For me, it was like I was dreaming or watching it all on MTV or something. The table where I was seated was one of the last ones he came to...and it's a good thing because I truly needed the time to compose myself (and find my lipstick and hairbrush!!!) :). Watching him talking, listening, smiling, hugging, and laughing with others...and getting nearer and nearer to me was....was......I cannot explain it.... I really can't put it into words.

Then.......he was walking toward our table. There were...I believe, 4 of us seated there. I cannot even remember for sure. Here we go.....

As he approached, he was looking at each one of us and had the sweetest, most gentle smile on his face. I'll never forget it. He was wearing a long coat....black tweed, as I recall it. I remember more how it felt than the details of what it looked like. He had his hair in a ponytail. He looked........wonderful. He smelled.......oh my gawd....so good - and I told him that when he hugged me and said "Hello", and then he said "Thank you!" very genuinely. He put out his hand as I introduced myself to him, and he asked me where I was from. I told him. And he asked me where exactly that was, and I told him. By this time, he has sat down in the chair next to me. He is giving me his undivided attention in this crowded, noisy, very excited room...And after 16 years of waiting for this moment, I was not going to waste a second of it! I looked him straight in the eyes right back and just started calmly (much to my own amazement) explaining to him how much it meant to meet him, how long I had loved and enjoyed the gift of his perfect voice, and how thankful I was that he was back. He was utterly gracious.....responding with appreciation as though he had never been told these things before. I'm thanking him, and he's thanking ME!

Frankly I cannot remember verbatim our conversation. I only remember that at one time I apologized for taking too much of his time; and he immediately responded that he was in no hurry, and that he had nothing but time!!!!! We also joked back and forth about a cute comment he made about his age (I wish I could remember it!!) That just stands out because the fact that Steve Perry and I once sat at a table in the SF Hard Rock Cafe joking and laughing together.....still blows me away.

He has an incredible way of putting one at ease immediately. Once the initial shock of him turning to me and me realizing THIS IS IT! passed, I felt wonderfully comfortable with him.....and fortunately the feelings in my heart flowed from my mouth without me stumbling over them.......which I had worried about, in my nervousness.

When Steve moved on to the table next to us, the back of the chair he sat down in bumped the back of my chair........(this is GREAT!!!) and we both turned around at the very same time in a way that his right and my left shoulder touched! When our eyes met, we both just laughed some more. He was so AWESOME, you guys!!!

One of the people at my table made an unhappy comment about how I had taken up all of Steve's time. I wanted to just laugh in all of my joy...but I realized she was really upset. I just explained to her that I was the last one at the table he had spoken to..........and that it just seemed we had stuff to talk about! I hadn't planned it! (But I surely was beyond happy and thankful about it!!!!)

This once-in-a-lifetime encounter with Steve would have been more than enough to hold me. But thanks to Lora and Cyndy, we would have one more opportunity to speak with Steve on this magical trip. Prior to Steve's show at the Warfield, we were told to come early to have pictures taken with Steve, and spend a little time with him before the show!!!!! At this point, I'm thinking "Pinch me! This can't be real!" But it was.

Once we were all inside, Steve walked on over to us with a big old "HI you guys!!!!!" We were all more comfortable and relaxed, having spent time with him at the Hard Rock....and he was in light spirits, in spite of the fact we ran late.....and they had to delay opening the doors of the Warfield to let everyone else in! Steve saw to it that he signed autographs for every one of us, and had a picture taken with each of us.

I was wearing my pink "Somewhere There's Hope" airbrushed shirt...and he signed it for me..."To Kay Love Steve Perry". It was so funny and sweet, because he was oh-so-carefully trying to sign it without his hand touching me ... inappropriately. Always the gentleman. He was too cute! I was just standing there reveling in the fact that Steve Perry's face was within inches of my own. (And yes, he smelled delicious again!)

When it was time for pictures, I was standing there just watching him pose with those before me in line...listening to the little comments and all the love he was receiving and returning, enjoying seeing him smile and laugh and joke. I was just so amazed and happy to be there. When the girl in front of me was done, Steve looked over. I was standing there hesitantly, waiting for the photographer to tell me to go ahead......and I heard the words every single Steve Perry fan would love to hear.....(deep breath). He opened his arms, smiled, and said to me....... *"Come here, Girl."*

On Thursday December 8th and Friday December 9th, 1994.....my dreams of finally meeting Steve Perry came true. 'Don't Stop Believin'!

Nora Tragianese
Lead Vocalist TRAG band

My first encounter with the amazing voice of Steve Perry was at a school dance, 1979...I was 12 years old. It was held in the Cafeteria; there was a big stage there, with a "DJ" Booth set up in the middle, and 2 huge speakers set up on the left & right-hand corners.

They were playing all the popular records of the day; kids were dancing, etc...

...and then, I heard a slow, vamp-sounding blues riff....and then:*"...You make me weep...and wanna die..."*

To this DAY, I can remember turning around, as if in a trance, and I just stood there, staring at the speaker, thinking to myself, *"WHO is THAT?!"*

Everything fell to the wayside; it was just me, the music, and that VOICE...I never heard anything like it before! And the fact that a MAN'S voice could sound like that was just incredible! Wow...

Fast-forward to May, 1983:

I was 15 years old, and hanging out with my older sister and her gang of friends...she asked me if I wanted to go with them to the Hartford Civic Center to see Journey's show during their "Frontiers" tour. Now, this is where it gets weird...because we had NO

TICKETS!! So, I agreed; we all piled into Brian's car and made the hour-trip to Hartford...Brian, the oldest at 18, negotiated with a ticket-scalper, and managed to get all of us tickets........in section 213 row MM!!!

Oh my God...Brian was cursing his head off all the way up to our seats...and when I say "up", I mean, "UP"! We were on the ceiling....to give you an idea of how far up, just visualize this: when I stood up, the top of the seat in front of me was only up to my mid-shin! And, there was "sticky stuff" all over the floor; to keep you rooted in place...it was a sheer drop!!

So finally, after Bryan Adams, the show started.....they were all the size of ants....thank God for those projection screens; they made a world of difference...they started out with "Chain Reaction".....the energy, sound, lights, performance...everything was amazing. After 2 or 3 songs, Steve stopped to greet the audience...people went WILD! He asked for the house lights to be turned up - *"I CAN HEAR YOU, BUT I CAN'T SEE YOU!!!"* he yelled. When the lights came up, people went even crazier!!

Then, he said this: *"Yeah; OK - I can see all you people down HERE....BUT, WHAT ABOUT THE PEOPLE UP THERE?!?!"* and pointed up to the upper decks. All the lights went out...a big, Hollywood-style Klieg-light snapped on at the bottom of the stage, swung around, and it hit right on OUR row!!!

I waited for it to reach me, and when it did, I made the most out of my few seconds...I jumped up and down and waved like a MANIAC....right then, Steve put his hand over his eyes to shield them from the lights, and waved back!!!!

Oh my God – I lost it!! - it was like my "Beatlemania"!!

The rest of the show blew me away even more....near the end, they played "Rubicon" - on the last phrase of the song *"Opportunity is yours"*, he was pointing all over the place...then, on the last "YOURS!", he ran over to our side, and pointed up - and I swear - in my 15-year-old mind, he pointed right at ME!

Something changed in me that night...I felt like somehow, I was "watching my future".......from that night on, I knew what I wanted to do with my life: I was going to be a singer.

Fast-forward, again, to 1994...and to more "strange coincidences": I lost my job in CT; found another one in New York State. In one of their local newspapers, I saw a display-ad for STEVE PERRY, of all people: His Solo Tour was coming to a venue in Poughkeepsie, NY - after that, he was scheduled to come to New Haven, CT. "Something" told me to get the tickets for the

NY show, so I did.

Good thing, too.....he never made it to CT. So, I bought the tickets...and this time around, they were better than I'd hoped for: sixth row!!! YES! FINALLY!!

It was in a renovated, old-fashioned, intimate theater...literally an "up close an personal" evening....So much nicer than 1983.

During the beginning of "Listen To Your Heart", he ran over to our side, stood right where we were sitting, and sang the first line: *"We were both together, naturally; I was lovin' you, babe...you were lovin' me..."*

I was singing right along with him - I pointed at him; pointed at me...I made him smile! I couldn't believe it!

Near the end, I noticed that people were running up to rush the stage, and no-one stopped them...so, I said to myself, "It's now or never...if you don't do this, you'll be KICKING YOURSELF the rest of your life!!" So, I got up, climbed over chairs, people - anything

and everything to get to the stage. I ran over to the right-hand side; Steve's left...I was so close, I could've untied one of his work boots. During a guitar solo, Steve was looking at everyone - and I mean EVERYONE: there was approx. 30 people in the crowd...then, he looked at me...and he did a double-take! I don't know why he did, but he did...I tried to be so cool about it, but I kind of freaked out - my eyes went wide, and I looked away and down...I looked back up, and he was still looking at me! So, I smiled and nodded at him.

There was so much I wanted to say to him...what do you say when your "life's-inspiration" is looking at you squarely in the eye? I mean, there was absolutely no way on Earth that he knew that I was that 15-year-old girl with stars in her eyes when the spotlight hit her...

I could not believe I was close enough to look into his eyes that night!

Debbie

I started listening to Journey when "Infinity" came out. I was 14 or 15 years old. My friend had an 8-track (yes, an 8-track!). I popped it in and fell in love with this voice. I had never seen the band but I just remember how the voice captivated me. In that instant I was forever hooked. I went to every show, camping out for tickets, always trying to get up close but never could. I lived in Memphis at the time. Through the years I followed the band, bought every album, watching the Don Kirschner's rock concerts on TV, listening to every special (remember the King Biscuit Flour Hour?) and live concerts on the radio. I never thought that 15 years later I would actually get to meet him and shake his hand!!

It was the For The Love Of Strange Medicine tour; he was solo with his own back up musicians. It was at the Orpheum Theatre, a small venue - which was great. A friend from work told me he could get me front row- of course I didn't believe him, I mean, it was Steve Perry, someone I had adored for years. I am just not that lucky! Well, my friend came to work holding two front row tickets!!! I could not believe it!!

I took roses to the show with me since I was going to be close. During the show, people were lining up to give their flowers to Steve but since he was on stage, the security guards started taking the flowers from the fans and laying them on the stage. Steve finally said, "I am going to get my own flowers", He came down and took flowers and hugged everyone. I was on the other side and could not get over to the line of people. He got back on stage, I stood up with my flowers and he came back down to me! He took my flowers and I kissed him on the cheek! I could not believe it was me doing it. I talked one of the security guards in to letting my friend and I backstage after the show... it worked!!!!! They took us to a small room where there were several other people.

It was when the band members came in and started signing autographs that I realized I had no paper!! I took a show itinerary off the wall and they all signed it. I was waiting right by the door when Steve Perry walked in. He stood there, right in front of me... I could not believe it! Was I dreaming? He said "hello" to us all. I gave him the paper to sign and he looked at it and said, *"Did you sign it?"* I said, *"No, I want you to sign it"*. He said, *"I thought you were going to sign it?"*. So charming and funny! He gave me his autograph, worked his way around the room and back to the door, again right in front of me. I asked him about a song "If You Need Me, Call Me" and he told me it was on his new CD that was coming out. I looked right in to his eyes, told him how incredible it was to meet him and shook his hand... he said, *"It's nice to meet you too"*. I could have died that night!

It was an experience that still gives me chills to talk about to this day.

Caryn Stevens

I fell in love with Journey and Steve Perry in late 1981/82. I can't tell you why, to this day, but when I saw the advertisement on TV for their Houston Texas Summit concert, I decided to tape it. When I finally played it back, I sat transfixed, staring at the TV. My senses were on overload. Here was one of the most beautiful men I had ever seen with the most beautiful voice I'd ever heard. I started it over and played it again…and again…and again. From then on, all I wanted was MORE!

Journey was the hottest band at the time, so I was able to watch them all the time on MTV and listen to their albums until the tapes wore out, but I craved the real thing. To be in the same room with "The Voice" would be a dream come true.

FINALLY they would be playing live! It was August, 1983. I called any and all of my friends I thought would be willing to spend serious money on tickets, because I was not going to have nose-bleed seats. I would be up-front, as close to him as I could get! I was a starving high-school student, so my mom helped fund my Journey habit and offered to chauffer me and my friends to the concerts.

They were playing August 5, 6, 7, 9 and 10th at the Los Angeles Forum. Now, you have to understand that this venue seats between 16,000 and 18,000 people! They were playing FIVE nights! There aren't many bands who could do that, even now.

I went four out of the five nights. I even snuck a camera in one night and he looked directly at me. I was in heaven. I think Frontiers is their most adventurous album, and I was in ecstasy to hear most of the songs performed live with his flawless voice.

If a band is good in concert (and Journey is awesome) it makes the addiction even worse. I knew I had to wait patiently for them to put out another album and tour again. I satisfied myself once again with albums, MTV and stacks of "Circus" magazine. I went to "Record Meets" where you buy memorabilia of your favorite rock stars and I spent much of my hard-earned money there.

I was rewarded for my loyalty. It took three years, but they finally put out the album. "Raised on Radio" in 1986 and were going to tour! I called up the ticket broker and told him "I want seats ON the stage". He happily obliged. I would be front row center.

I did see Journey when Randy Jackson of "American Idol" fame was playing bass in his spandex pants! I'm glad I have the tour program to remind me of that, however, because the only part of my face the other band members saw was my profile. My friend told me Neal was staring at us and I didn't even know it. All I could see was *him*. I watched Steve Perry glide across the stage, working his magic to make the crowd go wild.

At one point he was over by the drums with his back to the audience, doing that dance he always does, when suddenly he turned around and our eyes met. I know "time stood still" is such a cliché, but it really did. I was dancing, swaying back and forth to the music. He began to sway in time with me, looking into my eyes. That moment is frozen in time. My mind took a picture and it will be with me always.

I didn't realize it would be the last time I'd see Journey live, with Steve Perry. It breaks my heart.

I had never gotten to meet him. In 1994, right before the release of his album "For the Love of Strange Medicine" I worked at a movie studio that shares the same name with his record label. It turns out he came to the commissary (the cafeteria on the studio lot) on the one day I didn't go. Another girl I was working with who was a HUGE fan did wind up going that day. When she showed me the autograph I was green with envy.

It would be a long time before I finally got to meet him. It finally happened a few years ago. Unfortunately, I was with my boss and a co-worker at a nice restaurant. I tried to act "cool" as we walked past his table on the way out to the patio, and realized it was HIM. I tried not to stare at the back of his head and profile as I attempted to eat and actually taste my food, but couldn't. I finally said, "I think that's Steve Perry". Cool. Calm. "The sun used to rise and set above that man's head." Obviously I wasn't playing it as cool as I thought, because my boss commented that she had never seen me quite like this before.

They tried to encourage me to get his autograph, but I said I didn't want to bother him while he was eating. If he got mad at me, I couldn't live with myself.

We actually left, me looking back longingly at where he sat. We were out on the street when my co-worker yelled STOP! You have to do this! I'll go, but you have to come with me! We walked back inside. She double-checked with the hostess who confirmed that yes it was indeed Steve Perry. My co-worker grabbed the business card for the restaurant and marched bravely forward. I followed, barely aware of my own existence as I floated slowly towards his table. I got there just in time for him to say "is this for you or for you?" pointing to me. I finally found my vocal chords and said, "it's for me." I actually told him I didn't want to bother him while he was eating! He expressed his appreciation and said, "What's your name?" I was proud of myself for remembering it! While he was writing the autograph, I was thinking "HE'S SITTING RIGHT HERE, IN FRONT OF YOU! SAY SOMETHING! I wracked my brain. Here I was, in the presence of the man I'd been in love with for twenty years and I couldn't think of what to say! I settled for, "I've listened to you all my life and I think you're awesome" which in retrospect, at least didn't make me look like the blathering idiot I was inside, but didn't begin to express the huge burst of joy and happiness he brought to the dull life of a shy, awkward high school girl. He again expressed his appreciation, handed me back the card and shook my hand. If he had been standing up, I would have requested a hug.

We got back outside and I hugged my co-worker so hard, her eyes bulged out of her head! She said it was the best hug she'd ever gotten. I cried like a baby and requested the pen to keep (it was my boss'). So much for acting "cool". I couldn't work or do anything the rest of the day.

If I'm lucky enough to see him again, I'm going to get on my knees and beg him to get back on the stage, where he belongs.

Christine

In 1983 I was in High School. A group of us planned to go see Journey. The day before the concert, I realized it was going to be just me and the guy driving to the concert. I backed out. I didn't know him well, and figured I'd catch the next concert, as I was an avid Steve Perry fan. I was crushed when the band broke up. I drove my friends and family nuts with my obsession with Steve. I liked Journey, but STEVE was JOURNEY!

1994. I'm married, 3 little boys and one on the way. Steve Perry is coming to the Rochester Auditorium Theatre in November 94. My Birthday is 11/19, so my husband bought tickets. I was ECSTATIC! The day of the concert, there was news on the radio that Steve had gotten sick, and wouldn't be performing. The concert would be rescheduled. It was the WORST B-Day of my life. I cried for 2 days. I was a 26 year old woman crying over Steve.

Anyway....January 1995, Steve is COMING! I was so excited. Keep in mind…by now, I'm 7 months pregnant! My husband and I arrive at the Rochester Auditorium Theatre. I could hardly stand the wait. FINALLY out came Steve…T-Shirt, torn jeans, flannel shirt, and work boots! Hair in a ponytail. I screamed so loud my throat hurt!

About halfway through his performance, I went down to the front corner of the stage. A security guard was sitting there, and wouldn't let me get any closer, and as I was arguing, Steve started toward my corner of the stage. He didn't come all the way over, but far enough for me to almost faint!!! That was one of the highlights of my life!

2 months later my son was born, and I named him Aaron RAY! Ray is Steve Perry's middle name!

I'm now 35 years old, and still obsessed. I have a Journey DVD that I watch almost daily, and my 5 year old daughter knows all the members of the band, and she LOVES Steve Perry! She sings along with him, and knows all of the hand gestures for all of the songs! I still drive my friends and family insane over my obsession, but Steve Perry is the hottest, sexiest man alive!!

That's my story. I saw him perform, and would definitely see him again given half a chance!!

The first concert I ever went to was in 1980, Gregg Rolie was in the band, and The Baby's opened for them. It was at the Oakland Coliseum Complex. The concert was indoors. It was a magical time. Steve had command of the stage, running all over it, and Journey was giving the fans one hell of a show! I can't remember the set list, but boy, was I blown away watching them. I didn't have a front row seat, mine was off to the side, and this was before they invented the big screens that they used later on. But still, you could feel the energy Steve gave off!!

The second and third concerts, and maybe a fourth is in there, I can't remember, was again at the Oakland Coliseum, but in the outdoor complex. Those concerts were called "Days On The Green". They would have other acts on first, finishing with Journey. By then, they had the big screens, so everyone could see the band. Now the whole outdoor complex was filled from top to bottom with fans. You could move around, since there was no assigned seating like the first concert I went to. I moved around quite a bit. When nighttime fell, you could feel the anticipation of the crowd, knowing that soon, Journey would be onstage. Then you could hear the opening music, and then the band took the stage. You could hear the roar of the fans, starting from the very front, moving along to the whole complex. The whole place roared with excitement! Seeing Steve and Journey under the stars is a memory I will never forget. I also had bought some t-shirts from the various concerts, and I wish I still had them.

The last time I saw Journey with Steve Perry was in August of 1986 at Mountain Aire in Angels Camp, California. My ex-husband and I left for Angels Camp fairly early that morning.

It was a very hot ride. We drove up on Highway 4, and when we got close to Angels Camp, there was lots of traffic. We were stuck in traffic for hours, but it didn't bother us because we were going to see Journey. What is so unique about this memory is that the local residents of Angels Camp who lived on the Highway, would take their garden hoses and hose anyone off who wanted to cool down, or gave people water to drink.

We finally get to the Fairgrounds and there were masses of people there. What I didn't know at the time, but I would find out later is that there was going to be a filming crew there and the Journey concert was going to be videotaped. I later found this out when I saw the Greatest Hits DVD. The only other band I remember playing before Journey was The Outfield.

So there I was, with my ex-husband, sweating and waiting for Journey. We would see helicopters landing and taking off behind the stage; I believe the helicopters were bringing in and taking out the various acts.

The night was falling and, again, the anticipation of Journey taking the stage was huge. It is something you can't really describe; you just had to be there to feel it. I wasn't that close to the stage, but I could see that they had two other people playing with them. I found out later that it was Randy Jackson and Mike Baird. And their look was so different too!

Once again, Steve took command of the stage, and Journey blew everyone away! Song after song, the audience sang along with them. It was another magical time under the stars. But little did I know then - that would be the last time I would ever see Journey. But what I can remember will be forever in my mind and heart!

Susan Kathleen Newman

I was privileged to see Steve Perry, the former lead singer of the mega-group Journey, in concert for his For The Love Of Strange Medicine Tour. It was 1986 when Journey was in Atlanta for their Raised On Radio Tour. His vocals had matured, but he could still belt out the songs...old and new. What a fantastic show. Flash forward to 1994...I was working in a dead-end job, and I had just broken up with my boyfriend...Needless to say, I was feeling really defeated. My lovely brother, not wanting me to be sad, asked if I'd like to see Mr. Perry in concert. He was coming to Atlanta in November of that year.....he did not have to ask me twice. My answer was a resounding YES. Being a Steve Perry/Journey fan since 1978 (seeing them live for the first time in 1980, and many times since then), I wondered how his voice would sound, and what he looked like. Not having heard him sing live in 8 years, I looked at this as a positive experience.

Arriving early at the Fox Theatre (having an Egyptian motif...very apropos for SP/Journey), I purchased myself and brother FTLOSM memorabilia (got to have the shirts and programs you know). We were seated in the Orchestra (center), about 8 rows back...the excitement was building! I could not stop thanking my wonderful brother for doing such a selfless thing for me....I am blessed to have a brother that thoughtful and kind.

When I heard the music start, the anticipation was building throughout the theatre...the crowd started cheering. .it grew louder and louder. The stage was dark, and when the lights came up there HE was. I was overjoyed to see my favorite singer of all time again. My heart was pounding...the adrenaline was flowing. Boy, did he look good, with his hair so long (he wore it in a ponytail). His casual look made him appear down-to-earth and approachable. The band that was with him were new faces, but seemed they would compliment his vocals well. I immediately stood up (my brother and I would stand during the entire show). The first song he sang was "Only the Young".....when he started singing, my signature goose bumps returned...what a voice...as clear and distinctive as ever...I was in for a musical treat tonight!

His set list included songs from his 2 solo albums, Street Talk and For The Love of Strange Medicine, along with many classic Journey tunes. As he sang each song, especially the "oldies", it was fascinating to hear the entire auditorium sing along with him word-for-word. He was definitely getting the fans "fired up". In between the songs, he spoke to the crowd, thanking them for allowing HIM to come to their city, reminiscing about the songs and being the wonderful showman I remembered back in 1986. He knew the crowd came to hear the hits, and that's what he stressed throughout the show. It was ok, since being a long time Journey/SP fan; I was well versed with the older songs. I had never sung so much in my entire life...what a humbling experience to sing along with the great Steve Perry.

Steve was backed by a talented group of musicians, and his hits like "Wheel in the Sky," and "Lovin', Touchin', Squeezin'" (an excellent prequel to the song was his red tux coming down from the ceiling, he was squashing the many rumors, as he had an hilarious conversation back and forth with it). He then calmly took the tux off the hanger and slipped it on...he looked great in it...brought back memories of him wearing it during the ROR tour. He then turned his back to us, and proceeded to pull out the rubber band holding back his gorgeous to-the-waist hair. Turning around again, looking at the fans, he calmly handed his rubber band to one as a souvenir. It was a cool experience. My heart was beating so fast at that point, I wish I had been in the front row.

As he sang each song, the memories came flooding back, seeing him perform in front of thousands in the early and mid 80s. It's like he had never left...that we as the fans had held him in suspended animation.

The song, "Don't Stop Believin'", his first encore, brought the house down. We were whipped into a frenzy by the end of the night. We DID NOT want this evening to end. Sadly, the evening ended with the touching "Faithfully". Steve had thanked all his fans who had been there for him all these years, and I was crying at that point. It was as though I was watching an old friend walk away.

You guessed it - Steve Perry gets TWO THUMBS UP from me! The show was a memorable one, spotlighting the old and new, performed by the always recognizable Steve Perry. Steve is one of those special artists who really appreciates his fans...he was there to give them a show...and boy did he ever. I don't think there was a dry eye in the house. Those memories will last a lifetime. My brother and I thoroughly enjoyed the show. Actually, my brother then went out and bought all of Steve's CDs, both solo and Journey-related. I had converted another person to the "gospel" of Steve Perry.

Steve...thank you for providing your fans with many years of memorable music. You are definitely "The Voice". God Bless you...We love you...

The Fans.

The Mike Hausmann Picture Collection

Los Angeles Coliseum 1980

San Diego Sports Arena 1979

San Diego Sports Arena 1979

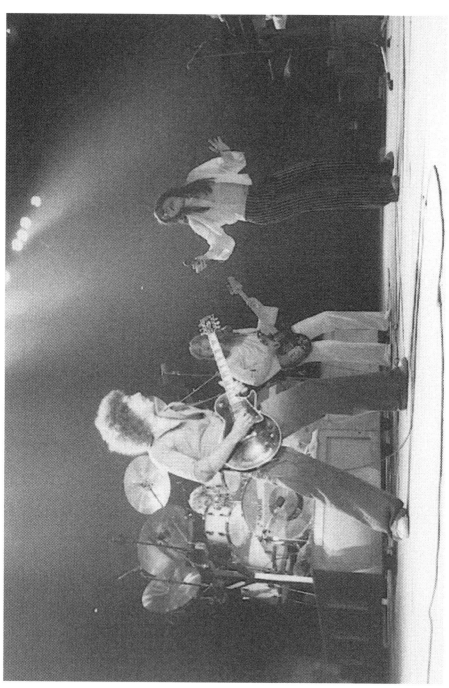

Long Beach Arena, California, 1979

Los Angeles Coliseum 1980

Los Angeles Coliseum 1980

Shot from onstage at a free concert at U.C. Berkeley, CA 1978

The making of "Lovin' Touchin' Squeezin'" video

Los Angeles Coliseum 1980

Los Angeles Coliseum 1980

The making of "Lovin' Touchin' Squeezin'" video

(California, 1978)

Discography and Collaborations

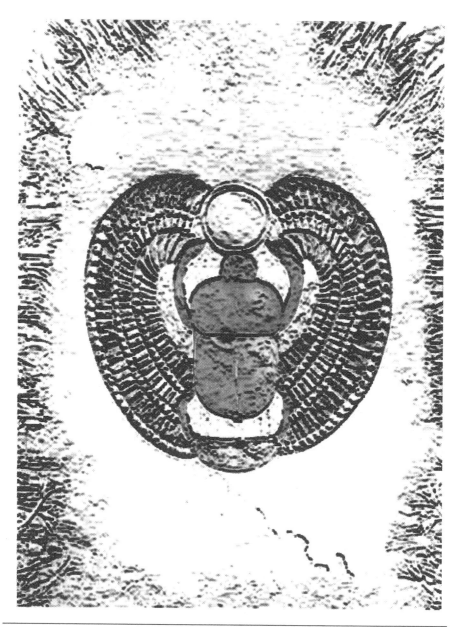

Steve Perry's Solo Albums:

Street Talk* (released: April 1984, Columbia)

Oh Sherrie

I Believe

Go Away

Foolish Heart

It's Only Love

She's Mine

You Should Be Happy

Running Alone

Captured By The Moment

Strung Out

* Personnel: Steve Perry (vocals); Michael Landau, Craig Hull, Billy Steele, Waddy Wachtel (guitar); Steve Douglas (saxophone); Billy Cuomo (piano, synthesizer) Randy Goodrum (Fender Rhodes piano); Steve Goldstein, Sterling Smith (keyboards); Duane Hitchings (synthesizer); Chuck Domanico (acoustic bass); Bob Glaub, Kevin McCormick, Brian Garafolo (bass); Larrie Londin (drums, percussion); Craig Krampf (drums).Producer: Steve Perry

Recorded at Record One, Los Angeles, California.

For The Love Of Strange Medicine* (released: July 1994, Columbia)

You Better

Wait Young Hearts Forever

I Am

Stand Up (Before It's Too Late)

For The Love Of Strange Medicine

Donna Please

Listen To Your Heart

Tuesday Heartache

Missing You

Somewhere There's Hope

Anyway

* Personnel: Steve Perry (vocals); Lincoln Brewster (guitar, background vocals); Michael Landau (guitar); Paul Taylor (keyboards, synthesizer, background vocals); Tim Miner (piano, keyboards, bass, background vocals); Larry Kimpel, Mike Porcaro, Phil Brown (bass); Moyes Lucas (drums, background vocals); Alexander Brown, Carmen Carter, Jean McLain (background vocals). Producers: Steve Perry, James "Jimbo" Barton, Tim Miner.

<u>Greatest Hits + 5 Unreleased</u>* (released: December 1998, Sony)

Oh Sherrie

Foolish Heart

She's Mine

Strung Out

Go Away

When You're In Love (For The First Time)

Against The Wall

Forever Right Or Wrong (Love's Like A River)

Summer Of Luv

Melody

Once In A Lifetime, Girl

What Was

You Better Wait

* Personnel: Steve Perry (vocals); Adrian Gurvitz (guitar, piano, keyboards, synthesizer); Mike Landau, Michael Thompson, Stevey DeLacey, Lincoln Brewster, Waddy Wachtel, Billy Steele, Craig Hull (guitar); Steve Douglas (saxophone); Randy Goodrum (piano, keyboards, drum programming); David Foster (piano, synthesizer, keyboards); Tim Miner (piano, synthesizer, bass); Bill Cuomo, Paul Taylor, Steve Goldstein, Sterling Smith, Scott Thurston (piano, synthesizer); Bob Glaub, Randy Jackson, Richard Michaels, Larry Kimpel, Chuck Domanico, Brian Garafalo (bass); Larrie London, John Robinson, Moyes Lucas, Jr., Craig Krampf (drums); Tony Brock (drum programming). Producers: Steve Perry, David Foster, Carol Bayer Sager, Randy Goodrum, Tim Miner.

<u>USA For Africa</u> (released: March 1985, Columbia)

B-side:" If Only For A Moment Girl" (Steve Perry)

<u>Quest For Camelot Soundtrack</u> (released: May 1998, Atlantic/WEA)

I Stand Alone
United We Stand

Journey Albums:

Infinity* (released: January 1978, Columbia)

Infinity
Lights
Feeling That Way
Anytime
La Do Da
Patiently
Wheel In The Sky
Somethin To Hide
Winds Of March
Can Do
Opened The Door

*Personnel: Steve Perry (vocals); Neal Schon (guitar); Gregg Rolie (keyboards); Ross Valory (bass); Aynsley Dunbar (drums).Producer: Roy Thomas Baker.

Evolution* (released: April 1979, Columbia)

Majestic
Too Late
Lovin, Touchin, Squeezin
City Of The Angels
When You're Alone (It Ain't Easy)
Sweet And Simple
Loving You Is Easy

Just The Same Way

Do You Recall

Daydream

Lady Luck

*Personnel: Steve Perry(lead vocals);Gregg Rolie (keyboards, vocals);Neal Schon(lead guitar, synthesizer guitar, vocals); Ross Valory(bass guitar, moog bass, vocals); Steve Smith (drums and percussion).Producer: Roy Thomas Baker. Recorded at Cherokee Studios, Los Angeles, California.

Departure* (released: March 1980, Columbia)

Any Way You Want It

Walks Like A Lady

Someday Soon

People And Places

Precious Time

Where Were You

I'm Cryin

Line Of Fire

Departure

Good Morning Girl

Stay Awhile

Homemade Love

*Personnel: Neal Schon (vocals, guitar); Gregg Rolie (vocals, harmonica, keyboards); Steve Perry (vocals); Ross Valory (bass, bass pedals, background vocals); Steve Smith (drums, percussion). Producers: Geoff Workman; Kevin Elson. Recorded at Automatt Studios, San Francisco, California.

Dream After Dream* (released: 1980, CBS Records Japan)

Destiny

Snow Theme

Sandcastles

A Few Coins

Moon Theme

When The Love Has Gone

Festival Dance

The Rape

Little Girl

*Personnel: Steve Perry – vocals; Neal Schon - guitar (acoustic/electric), vocals; Jonathan Cain - keyboards, vocals ;Steve Smith - drums & percussion, producer ;Ross Valory - bass, vocals. Produced by: Kevin Elson; Journey .Recorded at Shinonomachi Studios, Tokyo, Japan.

Captured* (released: February 1981, Columbia)

Majestic

Where Were You

Just The Same Way

Line Of Fire

Lights

Stay Awhile

Too Late

Dixie Highway

Feeling That Way

Anytime

Do You Recall

Walks Like A Lady

La Do Da

Lovin, Touchin, Squeezin

Wheel In The Sky

Any Way You Want It

The Party's Over

10/21/20

*Personnel: Steve Perry (vocals); Neal Schon (guitar); Gregg Rolie (keyboards); Ross Valory (bass); Steve Smith (drums). Recorded at various locations during Journey's 1980 -Infinity Tour." Producer: Kevin Elson.

Escape* (released: August 1981, Columbia)

Don't Stop Believin

Stone In Love

Who's Crying Now

Keep On Runnin

Still They Ride

Escape

Lay It Down

Dead Or Alive

Mother Father

Open Arms

*Personnel: Steve Perry (vocals); Jonathan Cain (guitar, keyboards, background vocals); Neil Schon (guitar, background vocals); Ross Valory (bass, background vocals); Steve Smith (drums).

Producers: Mike Stone; Kevin Elson. Recorded at Fantasy Studios, Berkeley, California.

Frontiers* (released: February 1983, Columbia)

Separate Ways (Worlds Apart)

Send Her My Love

Chain Reaction

After The Fall

Faithfully

Edge Of The Blade

Troubled Child

Back Talk

Frontiers

Rubicon

*Personnel: Steve Perry (vocals); Neil Schon (guitar, background vocals); Jonathan Cain (keyboards); Ross Valory (bass); Steve Smith (drums). Producers: Mike Stone; Kevin Elson.

Recorded at Fantasy Studios, Berkeley, California.

Raised On Radio* (released: May 1986, Columbia)

Girl Can't Help It

Positive Touch

Suzanne

Be Good To Yourself

Once You Love Somebody

Happy To Give

Raised On Radio

I'll Be Alright Without You

It Could Have Been You

The Eyes Of A Woman

Why Can't This Night Go On Forever

*Personnel: Steve Perry (vocals); Neal Schon (guitar, background vocals); Jonathan Cain (keyboards, background vocals). Additional personnel: Randy Jackson (bass); Steve Smith, Larrie Londin (drums); Randy Goodrum (background vocals).Producer: Steve Perry.

Recorded at Plant Studios, Sausalito, California and Fantasy Studios, Berkeley, California.

Trial By Fire* (released: October 1996, Sony Music)

Message Of Love

One More

When You Love A Woman

If He Should Break Your Heart

Forever In Blue

Castles Burning

Don't Be Down On Me Baby

Still She Cries

Colors Of The Spirit

When I Think Of You

Easy To Fall

Can't Tame The Lion

It's Just The Rain

Trial By Fire

Baby I'm Leaving You

I Can See It In Your Eyes

*Personnel: Steve Perry (vocals); Jonathan Cain (acoustic guitar, keyboards, background vocals); Neal Schon (guitar, background vocals); Ross Valory (bass, background vocals); Steve Smith (drums).Additional personnel: Paulinho Da Costa (percussion); Scott "Click Cheese" Pinkerton (programming).Producer: Kevin Shirley.

Recorded at Ocean Way Recorders, Los Angeles, California, The Site and Wildhorse Studio, Marin County, California.

<u>Time 3 Box Set</u> * (released: September 1992, Columbia)

Time 1

Where Were You
Line of Fire
Homemade Love
Natural Thing
Lights
Stay Awhile
Walks Like A Lady
Lovin', Touchin', Squeezin'
Dixie Highway
Wheel In The Sky
The Party's Over (Hopelessly In Love)
Don't Stop Believin'
Stone In Love
Keep On Runnin'
Who's Cryin' Now
Still They Ride
Open Arms
Mother, Father

Time 2

Off A Lifetime
Kohoutek
I'm Gonna Leave You
Cookie Duster
Nickel And Dime
For You

Velvet Curtain/Feeling That Way

Anytime

Patiently

Good Times

Majestic

Too Late

Sweet And Simple

Just The Same Way

Little Girl

Any Way You Want It

Someday Soon

Good Morning Girl

Time3

La Raza Del Sol

Only Solutions

Liberty

Separate Ways (Worlds Apart)

Send Her My Love

Faithfully

After The Fall

All That Really Matters

The Eyes Of A Woman

Why Can't This Night Go On Forever

Once You Love Somebody

Happy To Give

Be Good To Yourself

Only The Young

Ask The Lonely

With A Tear (instrumental)

Into Your Arms (instrumental)

Girl Can't Help It

I'll Be Alright Without You

*Personnel: Steve Perry (vocals);Gregg Rolie (vocals, keyboards); Robert Fleischman(vocals); George Tickner, Neal Schon (guitar); Jonathan Cain (keyboards); Randy Jackson, Ross Valory (bass guitar); Mike Baird, Prairie Prince, Steve Smith, Aynsley Dunbar (drums).

Greatest Hits* (released: March 1998, Sony)

Only The Young

Don't Stop Believin

Wheel In The Sky

Faithfully

I'll Be Alright Without You

Any Way You Want It

Ask The Lonely

Who's Crying Now

Separate Ways (Worlds Apart)

Lights

Lovin, Touchin, Squeezin

Open Arms

Girl Can't Help It

Send Her My Love

Be Good To Yourself

*Personnel: Steve Perry (vocals); Neal Schon (guitar); Gregg Rolie, Jonathan Cain (keyboards); Ross Valory, Randy Jackson (bass); Steve Smith, Aynsley Dunbar, Larrie Londin (drums). Producers: Mike Stone, Roy Thomas Baker, Steve Perry, Geoffrey Workman, Kevin Elson.

Greatest Hits Live* (release: October 1998, Columbia)

Don't Stop Believin'

Separate Ways (Worlds Apart)

After The Fall

Lovin', Touchin', Squeezin'

Faithfully

Who's Cryin' Now

Any Way You Want It

Lights

Stay Awhile

Open Arms

Send Her My Love

Still They Ride

Stone In Love

Escape

Line of Fire

Wheel In The Sky

*Personnel: Steve Perry (vocals); Neal Schon (guitar, background vocals); Jonathan Cain (keyboards, background vocals); Ross Valory (bass, background vocals); Steve Smith (drums). Recorded between November 5, 1981 & July 19, 1983.

<u>Essential Journey</u>* (release: October 2001, Sony)

DISC 1

Only The Young - (from "Vision Quest")
Don't Stop Believin'
Wheel In The Sky
Faithfully
Anyway You Want It
Ask The Lonely - (from "Two Of A Kind")
Who's Crying Now
Separate Ways (Worlds Apart)
Lights
Lovin', Touchin', Squeezin'
Open Arms
Girl Can't Help It
Send Her My Love
When You Love A Woman
I'll Be Alright Without You
After The Fall

DISC 2

Chain Reaction
Message Of Love
Somethin' To Hide
Line Of Fire - (live)
Anytime
Stone In Love
Patiently
Good Morning Girl
Eyes Of A Woman, The
Be Good To Yourself
Still They Ride
Baby I'm A Leavin' You
Mother, Father
Just The Same Way
Escape
Party's Over, The (Hopelessly In Love)

* Personnel: Gregg Rolie (vocals, keyboards); Steve Perry (vocals); Neal Schon (guitar, background vocals); Jonathan Cain (keyboards, background vocals); Ross Valory (bass, background vocals); Randy Jackson (bass); Steve Smith, Aynsley Dunbar, Larrie London (drums).Producers: Steve Perry, Kevin Elson, Kevin Shirley, Mike Stone, Roy Thomas Baker.

Steve Perry's guest appearances and collaborations:

1979 – on "Sweet friction" (Ned Doheny - "Prone")

1980 – on "Love or Money", "The Iceman", "Heartbeat", "Run For Your Life" (Sammy Hagar -"Danger Zone")

1981 – on "Fast Life" (Tim Bogert -"Progressions")

1981 – on "Who's Right Or Wrong", "Drive My Car", "Yesterday's Gone", "Cold Hearted Woman" (Johnny Van Zant -"Round Two")

1982 – "Don't Fight It" – duet with Kenny Loggins ("High Adventure")

1983 – on "Self Defense" (Schon & Hammer - "No More Lies")

1984 – on "Can't fall Asleep To A Lullaby" (America - "Perspective")

1985 – on "We Are The World" (USA For Africa - "We Are the World")

1987 – on "Still In Love" (Sheena Easton - "No Sound But A Heart")

1988 – on "Soldiers Of Peace" (Crosby, Stills, Nash & Young - "American Dream")

1987 – on "White Fool" (Clannad -"Sirius")

1995 – on **"It's Over"** (Forrest McDonald - "I Need You")

1996 – on **"Primal"** (Jason Backer - "Perspective")

1997 – on **"I'll Always Remember"** (Jonathan Cain - "Body Language")

1999 – on **"Send my baby Home"** (Laidlaw - "First Big Picnic")

2000 – on **"I Wish You Were Mine", "An Angel Above Me"** (Tommy Tokioka - "Happy To Be Living")

2003 – on **"Can't Let You Go"** (Jeff Golub - "Soul Sessions")

2005 – on **"A Brand New Start"** (David Pack - "The Secret Of Moving On")

Bibliography:

16 Magazine (1981, 1982, 1983, 1984)

BAM (1981)

Circus (1978, 1980, 1983, 1984)

Classic Rock Revisited (2005)

Hit Parader (1978 – 1985)

Journey Force (1984, 1986, 1988)

Record Review (1981)

Rock & Rockline (1983, 1984)

Boston Globe (1994)

Crawdaddy Feature (1979)

Faces Rocks (1987)

Frontiers Magazine (1995)

Jam Magazine (1983)

LA Daily News (1994)

Music Express (1984)

USA Today (1997)

Wall Of Sound (1998)

Off The Record 2003- 2005 (Joe Benson)

Fan Asylum 2000 - 2006 (Lora Beard, Cyndi Poon)

Brave Words & Bloody Knuckles 2005 (Mitch Lafon)

CPSIA information can be obtained
at www.ICGtesting.com
Printed in the USA
BVHW032237020520
579092BV00001B/85